The New
One Pot
Cookbook

**More Than 200 Modern Recipes
for the Classic Easy Meal**

A **adams**media

AVON, MASSACHUSETTS

Published by
Adams Media, a division of F+W Media, Inc.
57 Littlefield Street, Avon, MA 02322. U.S.A.
www.adamsmedia.com

Contains material adapted from *The Everything® One-Pot Cookbook, 2nd Edition* by Pamela Rice Hahn,
copyright © 2009 by F+W Media, Inc., ISBN 10: 1-59869-836-2, ISBN 13: 978-1-59869-836-7.

ISBN 10: 1-5072-0025-0
ISBN 13: 978-1-5072-0025-4
eISBN 10: 1-5072-0026-9
eISBN 13: 978-1-5072-0026-1

Printed in the United States of America.

10   9   8   7   6   5   4   3   2   1

Library of Congress Cataloging-in-Publication Data

The new one pot cookbook.
Avon, Massachusetts: Adams Media, 2017.
Includes bibliographical references and index.
LCCN 2016027524 | ISBN 9781507200254 (pb) | ISBN 1507200250 (pb) | ISBN 9781507200261 (ebook) |
ISBN 1507200269 (ebook)
LCSH: One-dish meals. | Casserole cooking. | LCGFT: Cookbooks.
LCC TX840.O53 N49 2016 | DDC 641.82--dc23
LC record available at https://lccn.loc.gov/2016027524

Always follow safety and commonsense cooking protocol while using kitchen utensils, operating ovens and stoves, and handling uncooked food. If children are assisting in the preparation of any recipe, they should always be supervised by an adult.

Many of the designations used by manufacturers and sellers to distinguish their products are claimed as trademarks. Where those designations appear in this book and F+W Media, Inc. was aware of a trademark claim, the designations have been printed with initial capital letters.

Cover design by Sylvia McArdle.
Cover images © iStockphoto.com/monaMonash, Ratsanai, issalina;
Natalia Hubbert, Natali Myasnikova, monaMonash/123RF.
Interior images © 123RF and GettyImages.

This book is available at quantity discounts for bulk purchases.
For information, please call 1-800-289-0963.

Contents

CHAPTER 4

Salads and Sides 92

CHAPTER 5

Poultry Entrées

CHAPTER 6

Pork Entrées 155

CHAPTER 7

Beef Entrées 177

CHAPTER 8

Pasta and Rice Entrées 215

Introduction

What is the worst part about making a home-cooked meal? The mountain of dishes you have to do afterward! Luckily, this handy book will help you minimize your cleanup time so you can sit down and enjoy the delicious food you made. With *The New One Pot Cookbook* you can make homemade meals without all the mess.

Throughout this book you will find more than 200 easy recipes for mouthwatering dishes that cook in just one pot. You'll find recipes for breakfasts and brunch, soups, pastas, entrées, and more. And just because you are cooking in one pot, don't think your cooking options will be limited. From casseroles in the oven, to stir-fries on the stove, to tender meats in the slow cooker, and fabulously fast meals in the pressure cooker—there are so many ways to cook in one pot!

Once you taste dishes such as Thai-Inspired Chicken Soup, Roast Pork Loin with Apples and Potatoes, and Lobster Paella, each cooked in one pot with limited mess, you'll be hooked on the one pot philosophy.

Ready to save time and effort and still have mouthwatering meals your family and friends will love? Then let's get cooking!

CHAPTER 1

One Pot
Basics

There is a whole world of one pot meals for you to explore! Simplifying the cooking methods expedites your cooking and cleaning process and leaves you more time to savor your meals and enjoy the company of the people you eat them with. The recipes in this book were created for use in today's world, with an emphasis on making the main entrée in one pot—if not the entire meal. The one pot meal philosophy is meant to show you ways to serve great-tasting food in ways that save you time and effort. Whatever you do, this book aims to make your dining experience more pleasurable and easier on you.

The Cooking Methods

If you're cooking simply as a way to put a meal on the table in the quickest and easiest way possible, you'll find many recipes you can use in this book. If, on the other hand, you live to cook, you've probably amassed all sorts of gadgets and gizmos and immersed yourself in the process. There's something in this book for you, too. No matter how comfortable or uncomfortable you are in the kitchen, the recipes in this book address your needs, giving instructions on how to make great food using a variety of cooking methods, including the following:

- **Baking** involves putting the food that's in a baking pan or ovenproof casserole dish in a preheated oven; the food cooks by being surrounded by the hot, dry air of your oven. (In the case of a convection oven, it cooks by being surround by circulating hot, dry air.)
- **Braising** usually starts by browning a less expensive cut of meat in a pan on top of the stove and then covering the meat with a small amount of liquid, adding a lid or covering the pan, and slowly cooking it. Braising can take place on the stovetop, in the oven, or in a slow cooker. The slow-cooking process tenderizes the meat.
- **Poaching** is accomplished by gently simmering ingredients in broth, juice, water, wine, or other flavorful liquid until they're cooked through and tender.
- **Roasting**, like baking, is usually done in the oven, but generally at a higher oven temperature. Food can be roasted by putting it directly on a baking sheet or in a roasting pan; however, fattier cuts of meat are often roasted by placing the meat on a rack inside a roasting pan so that the rendered fat drips away during roasting. Better cuts of meat that don't require becoming tender during the cooking process are best suited for roasting.
- **Sautéing** is the method of quickly cooking small or thin pieces of food in some oil or butter that has been brought to temperature in a sauté pan over medium to medium-high heat. Alternatively, you can sauté in a good-quality nonstick pan without using added fat; instead use a little broth, nonstick cooking spray, or water in place of the oil or butter.
- **Steaming** is a cooking method that uses the steam from the cooking liquid to cook the food. In this cookbook, steaming ingredients or vegetables in a covered container placed in the microwave is sometimes suggested.
- **Stewing** is similar to braising in that food is slowly cooked in a liquid; however, stewing involves a larger liquid-to-food ratio. In other words, you use far more liquid when you're stewing food. Not surprising, this method is most often used to make stew.

- **Stir-frying** is a cooking process similar to sautéing that's used to cook larger, bite-sized pieces of meat or vegetables in oil; the cooking is done in a wok or deep nonstick frying pan.
- **Tempering** is the act of gradually increasing the temperature of one cooking ingredient by adding small amounts of a hotter ingredient to the first. For example, tempering beaten eggs by whisking small amounts of hot liquid into them before you add the eggs to the cooking pan allows them to be mixed into the dish; tempering prevents them from scrambling.

Slow Cooker

A slow cooker is one of the easiest options for today's busy cook. You add the ingredients, turn the cooker to the desired setting, and come back several hours later to a fully cooked meal.

The most efficient slow cookers have a removable stoneware cooking pot. The stoneware is good at holding the heat, you can remove the pot and serve the meal directly from it, and it's easier to clean because it can go into the dishwasher.

Programmable slow cookers such as Cuisinart's 4-quart and 6.5-quart slow cookers let you start the cooking process at one temperature and automatically switch to a different setting according to how you've programmed it. For example, if you haven't had time to thaw the foods you're putting in the cooker, you have the option of starting it out on high for a couple of hours and then switching it to low heat for the duration of the cooking time. When the cooking time is completed, the cooker automatically switches to the "keep warm" setting, which holds the food at serving temperature until you're ready to serve it.

The option of having a "keep warm" setting is important for foods that can scorch or take on an unpleasant taste or texture if they're cooked too long. For that reason, even if you don't buy a slow cooker with all the bells and whistles, at least look for one that lets you set a cooking time and then automatically switches over to a warm setting when the cooking time is done.

Oven

Food can be baked, braised, or roasted in an oven. Fixing food in the oven can be simple if you know a few tricks. If a recipe calls for you to bake something at a higher temperature than your pan recommends, simply adjust the temperature down and increase the baking time accordingly. Assuming that meat was room temperature when it went into the oven, the general rule is to add 2 minutes of cooking time per pound for each 25 degrees you lower the temperature. The colder the food is when it goes into the oven, the longer it'll take it to bake. Also consider that a roast placed on a rack in a roasting pan will bake (roast) faster than one set directly in a pan because the rack allows more hot air from the oven to circulate around the meat. Then there's the matter of whether or not the temperature inside your oven is the same as the temperature you set it to. Not taking such variables into consideration can result in exceeding the desired internal temperature of the meat, or a roast that's more well done than you like.

Help ensure that you roast your meat to the desired doneness by using a thermometer with a probe that goes into the food in the oven and is attached to a programmable unit that sits outside the oven. A thermometer's display unit shows the current internal temperature, and some models are even equipped with an alarm that goes off when the meat reaches the correct internal temperature.

There are other factors that can affect roasting time, such as the size and shape of the meat, the amount of fat and bone, and whether the meat was aged. The best way to ensure that meat is roasted to your liking is to use the suggested roasting time given in a recipe as a gauge to time when you can have your meal ready to serve, and use a thermometer so you'll know when it's actually ready.

The most important thing to keep in mind when you prepare foods in the oven is that each time you open the oven, it will take it some time to recover lost heat. An electric oven will take longer to recover than will a gas oven. Adding a pizza stone can help any oven retain heat when the oven door is open, or at least recover the heat you lose more quickly.

Stovetop

Foods cooked on top of the stove usually need a little more attention than those made using other methods. This is especially true if you're not accustomed to using your stove. Use the heat settings suggested in the recipes, but until you become familiar with the temperatures that are required to achieve the desired effect (such as maintaining a slow simmer, for example), plan on babysitting the pot on the stove. Having a pot boil dry can not only ruin a meal, but it can cause a fire.

The cooking vessels you use will make a difference, too. Food will burn more easily in an inexpensive nonstick skillet than it will in heavier cast-iron, multiclad stainless, or hard anodized steel cookware. How well your cooking pan conducts the heat will make a difference as to how high you set the burner temperature. But, with some practice, you'll soon learn the perfect heat settings for each of your pans. It might take a medium-high setting to sauté food in an inexpensive skillet and lots of stirring to prevent the food from burning, but you can accomplish the same task in your triple-ply nonstick stainless steel skillet when it's over medium-low heat, and with less frequent stirring.

On the flip side, a heavier pan will retain the heat longer once it's removed from the burner than will an inexpensive skillet, so food cooked to perfection in a heavier pan must be moved to a serving dish more quickly to prevent it from overcooking. This is especially true of foods like gravy that tend to thicken the longer they sit; gravy can turn from a succulent liquid to one big lump if it stays on the heat too long.

Once you've removed the meat and other ingredients you've cooked in the pan and rid the pan of any excess remaining fat, deglaze it by putting it over a medium-high heat and then adding enough cooking liquid to let you scrape up any browned bits stuck to the bottom of the pan. Following this step before you add the other ingredients for your sauce or gravy adds more flavor and color.

Stovetop cooking doesn't have to be intimidating. In fact, stovetop cooking methods such as stir-frying are some of the quickest and most versatile ways to prepare meals. With the right instructions, it's easy to fix delicious meals for you and your family.

Pressure Cooker

Pressure cookers cook food up to 70 percent faster than other methods because steam trapped in the pot builds up pressure, which creates a hotter cooking temperature. The tight seal on the cooker also helps seal in vitamins and minerals and prevents the cooker from boiling dry during the cooking process. Stovetop pressure cooker models do require you to pay a bit more attention than do programmable countertop models because you need to verify that your burner setting is sufficient (and not too high) to maintain the needed pressure. Using either type of cooker is a convenient and quick way to cook. Pressure cookers are especially good for foods that need to be tenderized by the cooking process, such as less expensive cuts of meat.

Today's pressure cookers have built-in safety features that prevent some of the problems (like an exploding cooker!) associated with earlier models. Locking the lid in place prevents anyone from removing it before the pressure in the cooker is released.

Rotisserie

There are several recipes in this book that call for using a rotisserie chicken that you bring home from the supermarket, enhance, and make your own. If you have a rotisserie accessory for your outdoor grill, you can prepare your own mouthwatering rotisserie chicken outdoors without heating up the oven.

Keep a few things in mind when you buy an already-prepared rotisserie chicken, including:

- Choose chicken with a large, full breast; it will have more meat and is less likely to have dried out under a heat lamp at the store.
- As soon as you get the chicken home, remove the skin and pull the chicken from the bone; the meat is easier to separate from the bone while the chicken is warm.
- Shred or cube any excess chicken; refrigerate or freeze it in cup-sized portions so that it's already measured for future use.
- Reheat the already-cooked meat slowly and on low heat to avoid cooking the meat any further.
- Always taste the chicken before you add it so you can adjust the seasonings (especially salt) called for in the recipe.

- Once you find a good place to purchase rotisserie chickens, ask the clerk for the best times to buy them so you'll know when the store has the largest selection that hasn't been standing under the heat lamps for a long time.

Once you remove the meat from a rotisserie chicken you can use the bones to make chicken broth. Here's how: Put the chicken bones in a large pot and add a few black peppercorns and rough-chopped vegetables such as onion, garlic, carrots, and celery. Cover with water, bring to a simmer, and cook 30 minutes. Strain and discard the bones and vegetables. Freeze leftover broth (skimmed of fat) in ice cube trays, and then transfer the cubes to a plastic freezer bag so that you always have broth ready in an instant.

Once the skin is removed, the average purchased rotisserie chicken will yield about 4 cups of shredded chicken. Typically that amounts to about 12 ounces of white meat and 8 ounces of dark meat.

CHAPTER 2

Breakfast
and
Brunch

Crustless Cottage Cheese Quiche

SERVES 4-6

1. Treat a microwave-safe 9" deep-dish pie pan with nonstick cooking spray. Add the eggs and whisk until fluffy. Stir in the cottage cheese. Add the flour, salt, baking powder, and butter, and mix well. Fold half of the cheese and the vegetables into the egg mixture.
2. Cover the filled pan with a paper towel to prevent splatters. Microwave 6 minutes. Let rest 1 minute, then remove the paper towel.
3. Top with remaining cheese. Sprinkle green onions over the cheese.
4. Microwave an additional 5 minutes or until the cheese is melted and the quiche is set.

Nonstick cooking spray
5 large eggs
8 ounces cottage cheese
¼ cup all-purpose flour
⅛ teaspoon salt
½ teaspoon baking powder
¼ cup butter, melted
½ pound Monterey jack cheese, grated
½ (10-ounce) package frozen vegetables, thawed
3 green onions, chopped

VARY THE VEGGIES

Vary the vegetables in this quiche according to your family's tastes. You can use something as simple as peas and carrots or as varied as your favorite stir-fry vegetable mix. Just be sure to thaw the frozen vegetables before you add them to the egg mixture.

Baked Cornmeal with Cheese and Eggs

SERVES 8

1. Preheat oven to 350°F.
2. Add the butter to a 9" × 13" nonstick baking pan, turning the pan to coat the bottom.
3. In a medium bowl, mix the cornmeal cubes with the sour cream until it reaches the consistency of thick cake batter. If it's too thick, add more sour cream. Add the jack cheese and half of the Cheddar; mix to combine. Spread the mixture across the bottom of the baking pan. Bake 15 minutes.
4. Remove the pan from the oven. Press the bottom of a small glass into the mush to make 8 equally spaced indentations across the pan. Crack an egg into each indentation. Top each egg with salt (if using) and pepper. Sprinkle the remaining Cheddar over the top.
5. Bake an additional 15 minutes or until the eggs are cooked to desired doneness and the cheese is melted. Cut into 8 wedges. Serve hot or at room temperature.

¼ cup butter, melted
3 cups cornmeal mush, chilled and cut into cubes
1 cup sour cream, or more if needed
1 cup grated Monterey jack cheese
1 cup grated Cheddar cheese, divided
8 large eggs
Salt to taste (optional)
Freshly ground black pepper to taste

CORNMEAL MUSH BY ANY OTHER NAME

Cornmeal mush is simply the countrified name for polenta. Like polenta, it's typically made with yellow cornmeal. Grits are a similar dish made with white cornmeal. Regardless of what you call it, this recipe is a great way to use leftover polenta or grits.

A Modern Take on Welsh Rarebit

SERVES 6

1. In a nonstick saucepan, melt the butter over medium heat and stir in the cayenne pepper or hot sauce and Worcestershire. Add the beer and bring to a simmer. Lower the heat to medium-low or low.
2. In a small bowl, toss the cheese with the cornstarch and dry mustard. Add it to the beer mixture. Cook over low heat until the cheese is melted, stirring occasionally (melting the cheese over a low temperature prevents it from separating into a greasy mess).
3. Place the toast on individual plates. Top each slice of toast with a tomato slice, crisscrossed bacon slices, and an egg. Top with the cheese sauce.

1 tablespoon butter
Pinch cayenne pepper or dash hot sauce
1 teaspoon Worcestershire sauce
2/3 cup warm beer (ale, porter, or stout)
1 pound sharp Cheddar cheese, grated
2 teaspoons cornstarch
1 teaspoon dry mustard
6 thick slices bread, toasted
6 slices tomato
12 slices bacon, cooked
6 large eggs, poached or fried

WELSH RAREBIT ALTERNATIVE

For an alternative recipe, substitute milk for the beer. Sauté a small chopped onion and 1 cup sliced mushrooms in butter, and stir into the sauce along with a 10 3/4-ounce can condensed cream of tomato soup; bring to temperature. To serve, arrange slices of hard-boiled egg over the toast and top with the sauce.

Baked Monte Cristo Brunch Casserole

SERVES 4-8

1. Preheat oven to 350°F.
2. Beat the eggs, milk, and salt, black pepper, cayenne pepper, and Dijon mustard together in a small, shallow bowl.
3. Spread butter over one side of each slice of bread, and spread the mayonnaise on the other side. Dip 4 slices of the bread into the egg mixture and assemble them butter-side down in a 13" × 9" baking pan.
4. Top 4 slices of bread with a slice of Swiss cheese, a slice of ham, and then another slice of Swiss cheese. Place the remaining 4 slices of bread on top, mayonnaise-side down.
5. Pour the remaining egg mixture over the top of the bread. Bake 40–45 minutes or until the cheese is melted and the eggs are set. Let rest 10 minutes before cutting into serving pieces.

4 large eggs
½ cup whole milk or heavy cream
Salt to taste
Freshly ground black pepper to taste
Dash cayenne pepper
Dijon mustard to taste
8 slices bread (challah or brioche)
8 teaspoons butter
8 teaspoons mayonnaise
8 slices Swiss cheese
4 thick slices cooked ham

Hash Brown Potatoes with Sausage and Apples

SERVES 4

1. Heat the oil and butter in a 10" seasoned cast-iron or non-stick skillet over medium heat. Add the hash brown potatoes and cook 8–10 minutes, stirring occasionally, until they are thawed and beginning to brown. Stir in the salt, pepper, and thyme. Use a wide metal spatula to press the potatoes down firmly in the pan.

2. Add the sausage and apple over the top of the potatoes. Cover and cook 10 minutes or until the apple is tender. Top with the toasted walnuts and drizzle with the maple syrup. Cook uncovered an additional 10 minutes or until the hash browns are lightly browned on the bottom.

3. Use a spatula to loosen the potatoes from the pan and slide the dish onto a serving platter or serve from the pan.

2 tablespoons olive oil
1 tablespoon butter
5 cups frozen shredded hash brown potatoes
Salt to taste
Freshly ground black pepper to taste
1½ teaspoons chopped fresh thyme
6 ounces cooked smoked sausage, coarsely chopped
1 medium apple, cut into thin slices
1–2 tablespoons chopped toasted walnuts
1–2 tablespoons maple syrup

RECIPE TWEAKS

Instead of using the sliced apple, you can toss the sausage with some apple butter before you add it atop the potatoes. Or, for an out-of-the-ordinary taste treat, use another fruit butter, like pear butter. Then add another flavor dimension by sprinkling some cinnamon over the dish when you add the nuts.

Ham and Cheese Corn Bread

SERVES 4–8

1. Preheat oven to 350°F.
2. Melt the butter or bacon grease in a 12" cast-iron or oven-proof skillet over medium heat. Add the onion, garlic, and chili powder, and sauté until the onion slices are transparent, about 5–7 minutes. Remove from the heat and stir in the peanuts and pepper. Stir to mix well. Allow pan to cool slightly.
3. Once the pan has cooled, add the corn bread mix, egg, and milk; combine with the other ingredients in the pan. Spread evenly over the bottom of the pan and top with the ham.
4. Bake 15 minutes or until the corn bread is still moist but a toothpick comes out clean. Top with the cheese and return to the oven; bake an additional 5 minutes or until the cheese is melted. Garnish with olives if desired.

2 tablespoons butter or bacon grease
1 large yellow onion, peeled and thinly sliced
1 large clove garlic, minced
¼ teaspoon chili powder
½ cup chopped unsalted peanuts
Freshly ground black pepper to taste
1 (10-ounce) package corn bread mix
1 large egg, beaten
½ cup whole milk
½ pound cooked ham
3 slices American cheese (or Swiss or Cheddar)
Sliced pimiento-stuffed olives (optional)

Veggie, Egg, and Cheese Casserole

SERVES 4–8

1. Preheat oven to 325°F if using a Pyrex pie pan or 350°F if using a metal pie pan.
2. Treat an ovenproof 9" deep-dish pie pan with nonstick cooking spray. Add the eggs and whisk until fluffy. Stir in the cottage cheese. Add the flour, salt, baking powder, and butter, and mix well. Fold the cheese and the vegetables into the egg mixture. Add the onion, shallot, or green onion, if using.
3. Bake 40–45 minutes or until the top is lightly browned. Let rest 10 minutes before cutting into wedges for serving.

Nonstick cooking spray
6 large eggs
1 pound cottage cheese
¼ cup all-purpose flour
⅛ teaspoon salt
½ teaspoon baking powder
¼ cup butter, melted
1 pound Cheddar cheese, grated
1 (12-ounce) package frozen vegetables, thawed
Chopped red onion, shallot, or green onion to taste

STRETCH OUT THE SERVINGS

The baked recipe will serve 4 as a standalone breakfast or brunch dish. To stretch it to 8 servings, serve it with some brown-and-serve sausages and toasted English muffins or bagels. Some good vegetables choices might be asparagus, yellow and white corn, and baby carrots. You could also add salsa or marinara sauce to the finished product if you desire.

Bacon, Broccoli, and Cheese Quiche

SERVES 4-8

1. Preheat oven to 350°F.
2. Spread the bacon evenly over the bottom of the pie crust. Top with the cheese. Place the broccoli over the bacon and cheese.
3. In a medium bowl, whisk the eggs together with the milk or cream, salt, and pepper. Carefully pour the egg mixture over the ingredients in the pie crust.
4. Bake 35–45 minutes or until the center of the pie is set. Let sit 10 minutes before slicing. Serve warm or at room temperature.

8 slices cooked bacon, chopped
1 (9") deep-dish frozen pie crust, thawed
½ cup grated Cheddar cheese
1 cup cooked broccoli florets
6 large eggs
¼ cup whole milk or heavy cream
Salt to taste
Freshly ground black pepper to taste

THE VERSATILE QUICHE

This quiche can easily be adapted to match whatever you happen to have in your refrigerator. Substitute other leftover vegetables or use American cheese slices instead of the Cheddar. Just keep in mind that the cooler the temperature of the filling, the longer it'll take the quiche to bake.

Quiche Lorraine with Spinach

SERVES 4–8

1. Preheat oven to 350°F.
2. In a medium bowl, beat the eggs with the flour, then stir in the milk. Add salt, pepper, cayenne, mustard, and mayonnaise, if using. Fold in the cheese, bacon, and spinach. Pour into the pie shell.
3. Place the pie shell on a baking sheet or jellyroll pan and put in the oven. Bake 40–45 minutes or until the eggs are set. Let rest 10 minutes before cutting into wedges. Serve warm or at room temperature.

6 large eggs
1 tablespoon all-purpose flour
1 cup whole milk
Salt to taste (optional)
Freshly ground black pepper to taste (optional)
Dash cayenne pepper to taste (optional)
½ teaspoon Dijon mustard (optional)
1 tablespoon mayonnaise (optional)
½ pound Swiss cheese, grated
½ pound cooked bacon, cut into pieces
1 cup finely chopped fresh spinach
1 (9") unbaked pie shell

Basic Frittata

SERVES 4

1. In a medium bowl, whisk the eggs with the water, salt, and pepper. Bring a 10" ovenproof, nonstick skillet to temperature over medium-high heat, then add the oil and butter. Once the butter is melted and starts to foam, pour in the egg mixture. Tilt the pan to distribute the mixture evenly around the pan.

2. Lower the heat to medium and continue to cook until the eggs begin to set, occasionally tilting the pan to move any uncooked egg mixture evenly across it. Once the eggs start to set, distribute the toppings across the entire top of the frittata.

3. Place the pan in the oven and broil until the eggs are set and the cheese is melted and begins to bubble. Remove from the broiler and let the frittata rest 2 minutes. Slice as a pie and serve hot or at room temperature.

6 large eggs, at room temperature
2 tablespoons water
Salt to taste
Freshly ground black pepper to taste
$\frac{1}{2}$ tablespoon peanut or vegetable oil
$\frac{1}{2}$ tablespoon butter
Cheese, cooked meat, or vegetables for toppings

FRITTA-WHAT?

A frittata is basically an unfolded omelet that's topped with precooked meat, vegetables, and cheese and then finished under the broiler. That finishing step allows you to add a bit more filling than you can to an omelet. You could also stretch this frittata to 8 servings if you serve it with a salad.

Asparagus and Fontina Frittata

SERVES 6

1. Whisk the eggs, cream, salt, and pepper together in a medium bowl and set aside until needed.
2. Heat a 10" ovenproof, nonstick skillet over medium heat, then add the oil and the butter. Once the butter is melted, add the asparagus and sauté until crisp-tender, about 2 minutes. Increase the heat to medium-high. Add the tomato and sauté 2 minutes longer. Pour the egg mixture over the asparagus mixture and cook until the eggs begin to set. Sprinkle with the cheese. Reduce heat to medium-low and cook an additional 2 minutes.
3. Place the skillet under the broiler. Broil until the eggs are set and the cheese is golden brown on top, about 5 minutes. Remove from the broiler and let the frittata rest 2 minutes. Slice as a pie and serve.

6 large eggs
2 tablespoons whipping cream
1/2 teaspoon salt
1/4 teaspoon freshly ground black pepper
1 tablespoon olive oil
1 tablespoon butter
1 pound asparagus, trimmed and cut into 1/4–1/2" pieces
1 medium tomato, seeded and diced
3 ounces fontina cheese, diced

The Classic Omelet

1. In a small bowl, whisk the eggs with the water or cream and salt and pepper. Bring a 10" nonstick skillet to temperature over medium-high heat, and then add the oil and the butter. Once the butter is melted and starts to foam, pour in the egg mixture. Tilt the pan to distribute the egg mixture evenly around the pan.

2. Lower the heat to medium and continue to cook until the eggs are almost set, occasionally tilting the pan to move any uncooked egg mixture evenly across the omelet. Once the eggs are almost set, distribute the fillings across the half of the omelet that's opposite from the skillet handle.

3. If necessary, use a spatula to loosen the edges of the omelet from the skillet. Give the pan a shake to ensure the omelet will slide out of the pan, then slide it onto a serving plate, using the pan to fold the omelet in half.

3 large eggs, at room temperature
1 tablespoon water or heavy cream
Salt to taste
Freshly ground black pepper to taste
½ tablespoon peanut or vegetable oil
½ tablespoon butter
Cheese, cooked meat, or vegetables of your choice for filling

Sausage and Pepper Scramble

SERVES 8

1. Preheat an electric skillet to medium-high or heat a deep 3½-quart nonstick sauté pan over medium-high heat and add the oil. Once the oil is heated, add the onion and bell pepper and sauté until the onion is transparent, about 5 minutes. Add the sausage and cook 5 minutes, or until browned, breaking it apart as it cooks. Remove any excess fat, if necessary, by carefully dabbing the pan with a paper towel. Add the hash browns and cook covered 10 minutes or until the hash browns are tender and the sausage is cooked through. Stir to combine well.

2. In a medium bowl, whisk together the eggs, water or heavy cream, hot sauce (if using), salt, and pepper. Remove the lid from the pan and pour the eggs over the sausage-potato mixture. Stir to combine and scramble the eggs until they begin to set. Add the cheese and continue to scramble until the eggs finish cooking and the cheese melts. If you prefer, instead of stirring the cheese into the mixture, you can top it with the cheese; then cover the skillet and continue to cook 1–2 minutes or until the cheese is melted. Serve immediately.

1 tablespoon extra-virgin olive oil
1 large yellow onion, peeled and diced
1 medium green bell pepper, seeded and diced
1 pound ground sausage
4 cups frozen hash brown potatoes
8 large eggs
¼ cup water or heavy cream
1–2 drops hot sauce
Salt to taste
Freshly ground black pepper to taste
½ pound Cheddar cheese, grated

THE TIRED COOK'S PERFECT DISH

As long as you can position it so the cord is safely out of the way, you can fix this meal in an electric skillet at the table. Chop the vegetables the night before and mix the eggs together in a jar with a tight lid. You'll be able to sit down to cook while you savor your first cup of coffee.

Turkey-Topped Eggs Benedict

SERVES 1-2

1. While you toast the muffin, put the water and vinegar in a microwave-safe bowl. Crack the eggs into the water. Pierce each egg yolk with a toothpick. Cover the bowl with plastic wrap. Microwave on high 1½ minutes or until the eggs are done as desired. Keep in mind that as long as the egg remains in the water, it will continue to cook, so be ready to assemble the dish quickly.
2. To make the mock hollandaise, in a small bowl mix the yogurt, lemon juice, and mustard (if using).
3. To assemble the open-face sandwiches, place the toasted English muffin halves on a plate. Arrange lettuce atop the muffins. Top the lettuce with the avocado slices and then the turkey.
4. Use a slotted spoon to remove the eggs from the water and place them on top of the turkey. Salt and pepper the eggs to taste. Spoon the yogurt sauce over the eggs. Serve immediately.

1 English muffin, split
⅔ cup water
⅛ teaspoon white vinegar
2 large eggs
¼ cup plain yogurt
2 teaspoons lemon juice
¼ teaspoon Dijon or honey mustard (optional)
Lettuce leaves
½ medium avocado, peeled and sliced
4 ounces cooked turkey, heated
Salt to taste
Freshly ground black pepper to taste

Slow-Cooked Irish Oatmeal with Fruit

SERVES 8-10

1. Add the oats, water, apple juice, cranberries, raisins, apricots, maple syrup, cinnamon, and salt to a 4-quart slow cooker and stir to mix.
2. Cover and cook on low 6–7 hours or on high 3–3½ hours.
3. If desired, serve the oatmeal warm topped with brown sugar, chopped nuts, and milk, half-and-half, or heavy cream.

2 cups steel-cut Irish oats
5 cups water
1 cup apple juice
¼ cup dried cranberries
¼ cup golden raisins
¼ cup chopped dried apricots
¼ cup maple syrup
1 teaspoon ground cinnamon
½ teaspoon salt
Brown sugar to taste (optional)
Chopped toasted walnuts or pecans to taste (optional)
Milk, half-and-half, or heavy cream to taste (optional)

COOKING AHEAD

Once the oatmeal has cooled, divide any leftovers into single-serving, microwave-safe containers and freeze. When you're ready to eat, put a single serving in the microwave to defrost. Cover the container with a paper towel to catch any splatters, then microwave on high 1–2 minutes.

Homemade Granola

YIELDS 12 CUPS

1. Preheat oven to 250°F.
2. Add the oil and honey to a large microwave-safe bowl. Microwave until the oil is liquid and can be whisked into the honey. Mix in the oats, coconut, almonds, and cashews using a wooden spoon to stir until all the dry ingredients are coated.
3. Pour the mixture onto a 13" × 18" × 1" sheet pan and spread out evenly. Bake 75 minutes or until the mixture turns a nice, even, golden brown, stirring with a spatula every 15 minutes.
4. Remove the granola from the oven and allow to cool, stirring occasionally. Toss with the apricots, figs, cherries, and cranberries. Store in an airtight container up to 2 weeks.

¾ cup coconut oil
½ cup honey
4 cups old-fashioned rolled oats
2 cups sweetened shredded coconut
2 cups slivered or whole almonds
1 cup raw, unsalted cashews
1½ cups small-diced dried apricots
1 cup small-diced dried figs
1 cup dried cherries
1 cup dried cranberries

ALTERNATE RECIPE: MAPLE-WALNUT GRANOLA

Substitute chopped walnuts for half of the almonds and the cashews. Use ½ cup maple syrup and ¼ cup light brown sugar instead of the honey and raisins instead of dried apricots.

Baked French Toast with Toasted-Pecan Syrup

SERVES 8-10

1. Slice the bread into 20 (1"-thick) slices. Generously butter a 9" × 13" flat baking dish with 1 tablespoon butter. Arrange the bread slices in two rows, overlapping the slices.
2. Whisk the eggs, cream, milk, sugar, vanilla, cinnamon, nutmeg, and salt until blended but not too bubbly. Pour the egg mixture evenly over all the bread slices. Cover the pan with plastic wrap or foil and refrigerate overnight.
3. The next day, preheat oven to 350°F. While oven is coming to temperature, remove the baking pan from the refrigerator so that the French toast mixture begins to come to room temperature.
4. In a small saucepan, melt the remaining butter and mix with the brown sugar, pecans, corn syrup, cinnamon, and nutmeg. Remove the foil or plastic wrap from the baking pan and spread the pecan mixture evenly over the bread. Bake uncovered 45 minutes or until puffed and lightly golden. Serve warm.

1 (16-ounce) loaf challah or brioche bread
3/4 cup butter, divided
8 large eggs
1 cup heavy cream
2 cups whole milk
2 tablespoons granulated sugar
1 tablespoon vanilla extract
1/2 teaspoon ground cinnamon
1/2 teaspoon ground nutmeg
Dash salt

TOPPING
1 packed cup light brown sugar
1 cup chopped pecans
2 tablespoons light corn syrup
1/2 teaspoon ground cinnamon
1/2 teaspoon ground nutmeg

Salmon and Spinach Quiche

SERVES 6–8

1. Preheat oven to 375°F. Bake the pie shell for 10 minutes.
2. Drain the salmon and remove any skin pieces if desired. Mash any salmon bones and mix them into the salmon. Spread the salmon in an even layer over the bottom of the partially baked pie shell.
3. Cook the spinach according to package directions; drain well. In a medium bowl, mix together the spinach, jack cheese, cream cheese, salt, and thyme. Spoon the spinach-cheese mixture evenly over the salmon.
4. Use the same bowl to mix together the eggs, milk, and mayonnaise (if using), and then pour it over the salmon-and-spinach mixture in the pie shell.
5. Bake 40–45 minutes. Remove from the oven and let stand 10 minutes before cutting and serving.

1 (10") pie shell
1 (15.5-ounce) can pink salmon
1 (10-ounce) package frozen chopped spinach
1½ cups grated Monterey jack cheese
1 (3-ounce) package cream cheese, softened
Salt to taste
½ teaspoon dried thyme, crushed
4 large eggs, lightly beaten
1 cup whole milk
1 tablespoon mayonnaise (optional)

SALMON IS SUPER

Because of the cooked bones, salmon is high in calcium. It is also an easily digestible protein high in heart-healthy omega-3 fatty acids, which also help lower cholesterol. It contains healthy amounts of vitamins A and B as well.

CHAPTER 3

Soups
and
Stews

Salmon Soup

SERVES 4

1. Add the broth, salmon, onion, salt, and pepper to a 3-quart saucepan. Bring to a boil over high heat. Reduce heat, cover, and simmer 15 minutes.
2. Add the spinach, cover, and cook another 5 minutes. Serve.

4 cups chicken broth
1 pound fresh or smoked salmon
1 medium yellow onion, peeled and thinly sliced
Salt to taste
1/8 teaspoon freshly ground black pepper
1 bunch fresh spinach, chopped

SMOKED SALMON ALTERNATIVES

If you use fresh salmon in this recipe but still want to add a smoky flavor to the dish, garnish each serving with some finely chopped crisp bacon. You can find smoked salmon everywhere from Costco to Whole Foods.

Shrimp and Artichoke Soup

SERVES 8

Add all ingredients except the salt and pepper to a large saucepan. Stir to combine. Bring to a simmer over medium heat; reduce heat and simmer uncovered 15 minutes. Taste for seasoning and add salt and pepper, if needed.

1 (10¾-ounce) can condensed cream of mushroom soup
1 (10¾-ounce) can condensed cream of celery soup
3¼ cups whole milk
1 (5-ounce) can shrimp, drained
1 cup peeled and finely shredded carrots
1 (14-ounce) can artichoke hearts, drained and chopped
½ teaspoon curry powder
Pinch allspice
¼ teaspoon onion powder
Salt to taste
Freshly ground black pepper to taste

Beef and Blackberry Soup

SERVES 6-8

1. Add the oil to a 6-quart Dutch oven and bring to temperature over medium heat. Add the celery and carrots; sauté 3–5 minutes or until tender. Add the onions and sauté until the onions are transparent, about 5 minutes.
2. Trim the fat from the roast and cut it into bite-sized pieces. Add the meat to the Dutch oven and brown it for a few minutes. Add the broth, water, honey, blackberries, sweet potatoes, salt, and pepper. Bring to a boil. Lower the heat, cover, and simmer 1 hour or until the meat is tender.
3. Add the potatoes, if using. Cover and simmer an additional 30 minutes or until the potatoes are cooked.

3 tablespoons peanut or extra-virgin olive oil
2 stalks celery, diced small
2 large carrots, peeled and diced small
1 large yellow onion, peeled and diced
1½ pounds boneless chuck roast
2 cups beef broth
2 cups water
1 tablespoon honey
1 cup blackberries
2 large sweet potatoes, peeled and diced
Salt to taste
Freshly ground black pepper to taste
2 large russet potatoes, peeled and diced (optional)

NAME GAME
A boneless "English-cut" chuck roast is the perfect cut to use in a slow-cooked beef dish; it cooks up to pull-apart tender. The boneless cut is sometimes called an English roll. That cut of chuck roast also can be referred to as a cross rib roast, cross rib pot roast, Boston cut, English-cut roast, English roast, thick rib roast, bread and butter cut, or beef chuck cross rib pot roast.

Chicken and Corn Soup with Mini Dumplings

SERVES 4-6

1. Melt the butter in a deep 3½-quart nonstick skillet or large saucepan over medium heat. Add the celery and carrot; sauté 3–5 minutes or until soft. Add the onion and sauté until transparent, about 5 minutes. Add the garlic and sauté an additional 30 seconds. Stir in the broth and corn. Lower the temperature and allow the soup to simmer while you mix up the dumplings.

2. In a small bowl, mix the egg together with the salt and enough flour to make a dry dough. Working with 1 table-spoon of the dough at a time, rub it between your hands over the pan so that pieces of the dough drop into the soup. After all the dumplings have been added to the pan, add the chicken and simmer an additional 10 minutes or until dumplings are tender.

3. Serve with slices of hard-boiled egg floating on top of the soup. Garnish with parsley if desired.

2 tablespoons butter
1 stalk celery, finely chopped
1 large carrot, peeled and finely chopped
1 small yellow onion, peeled and chopped
1 clove garlic, minced
4 cups chicken broth
1 (17-ounce) can creamed corn
1 large egg, beaten
Pinch salt
¾–1 cup all-purpose flour
1 cup shredded cooked chicken
2 large hard-boiled eggs, peeled and sliced
Chopped fresh flat-leaf parsley for garnish (optional)

Butternut Squash Soup with Kielbasa and Wild Rice

SERVES 6-8

1. Preheat oven to 400°F.
2. Cut the squash in half and remove the seeds. Place the squash halves skin-side down on a baking sheet and drizzle with 1 tablespoon oil; bake 1 hour. Remove from the oven and let cool completely. Peel the squash and add it to a blender or food processor along with 2 cups broth; purée until smooth and set aside.
3. Add the remaining 4 cups broth and ½ of the chopped onion to a Dutch oven and bring to a simmer over medium heat. Stir in the rice; cook 1 hour or until rice is tender and most of the liquid is absorbed, stirring occasionally with a fork. Remove rice from the pan and set aside.
4. Add remaining 1 tablespoon oil to the Dutch oven and bring it to temperature over medium heat. Add the kielbasa; brown 3 minutes. Add the remaining onion and corn; season with salt and pepper and sauté 3 minutes. Add the squash purée; reduce heat to medium-low, cover, and simmer 20 minutes, checking occasionally and adding water if needed.
5. Skim off any fat on the surface, stir in the rice, and continue to cook 10 minutes. Remove from heat and stir in the cream. Serve garnished with parsley if desired.

1 (1½–2-pound) butternut squash
2 tablespoons extra-virgin olive oil, divided
6 cups chicken broth, divided
1 large yellow onion, peeled and diced, divided
1 cup uncooked wild rice
1 pound kielbasa, cut into ¼" slices
1 (12–16-ounce) package frozen whole-kernel corn, thawed
Salt to taste
Freshly ground black pepper to taste
Water, as needed
1 cup heavy cream
1 tablespoon chopped fresh flat-leaf parsley (optional)

MICROWAVE-ROASTED BUTTERNUT SQUASH

Instead of baking the butternut squash, you can fix it in the microwave. Wash the squash, slice in half lengthwise, remove the seeds, and place it cut-side down in a shallow microwave-safe pan. Add water to about ¾" deep. Microwave on high 8–10 minutes or until the squash is tender.

Pumpkin and Corn Soup

SERVES 4-6

1. Melt the butter in a Dutch oven over medium heat. Add the celery and carrot; sauté 3–5 minutes or until tender. Add the onion and apple; sauté until the onion is transparent, about 5 minutes. Stir in the pumpkin and broth. Bring to a boil; reduce heat and simmer 10 minutes. Use a stick blender to purée the soup if you wish.
2. Add the corn and the ham (if using); simmer 8 minutes or until the corn is tender. Add salt and pepper to taste. Garnish with pumpkin seeds if desired.

2 tablespoons butter
1 stalk celery, finely diced
1 large carrot, peeled and finely diced
1 medium yellow onion, peeled and minced
1 medium apple, peeled, cored, and minced
1 (15-ounce) can pumpkin purée
3 cups chicken broth
1 (10-ounce) package frozen whole-kernel corn, thawed
Diced cooked ham to taste (optional)
Salt to taste
Freshly ground black pepper to taste
Toasted pumpkin seeds, shelled (optional)

PUMPKIN SOUP VARIATIONS

Omit the corn in this recipe and stir in $1/2$ cup peanut butter and a little brown sugar instead. Or, season the soup by adding 1 teaspoon smoked paprika, $1/8$ teaspoon ground cumin, and a pinch of cayenne pepper. Turn any variation into a cream soup by stirring in $1/2$ cup heavy cream, or more to taste.

Thai-Inspired Chicken Soup

SERVES 6-8

1. Add the broth, ginger, garlic, shallots, and lime leaves to a 6-quart Dutch oven. Bring to a boil over medium heat. Peel the bottom 5" of the lemongrass stalks, chop, and add to the broth. Reduce heat, cover, and simmer 10 minutes. Strain the broth and discard the solids.

2. Return broth to the pan. Stir in the curry paste, sugar, coconut milk, and fish sauce. Bring to a simmer over low heat. Add the chicken, peppers, and lime juice. Cover and simmer 10 minutes or until the peppers are tender. Add salt and pepper to taste. Serve garnished with the cilantro if desired.

6 cups chicken broth
½" piece fresh ginger, thinly sliced
2 cloves garlic, minced
3 shallots, peeled and sliced
7 dried kaffir lime leaves
3 stalks fresh lemongrass
1 teaspoon Thai red curry paste
1 tablespoon granulated sugar
1 (14-ounce) can coconut milk
3 tablespoons Thai fish sauce
2 cups diced cooked chicken breast
2 small jalapeño peppers, seeded and thinly sliced
2 tablespoons fresh lime juice
Salt to taste
Freshly ground black pepper to taste
Chopped fresh cilantro to taste (optional)

Fish Soup with Lettuce

SERVES 4

1. Add the peanut oil to a deep 3½-quart nonstick skillet or wok and bring to temperature over medium heat. Add the garlic and stir-fry 30 seconds. Add the broth and bring to a simmer. Add the ginger and fish, cover, and simmer 5 minutes.
2. Use a slotted spoon to remove the ginger slices, and stir in the lettuce. Cook another 2 minutes. Add the salt, soy sauce, and toasted sesame oil to taste. Garnish with the chopped green onions.

1 tablespoon peanut oil
2 cloves garlic, minced
4 cups chicken broth
½" piece fresh ginger, thinly sliced
1 pound whitefish fillet, sliced thin
1 large head iceberg lettuce, chopped
Salt to taste
Soy sauce to taste
Toasted sesame oil to taste
3 green onions, chopped

Enchilada Chili

SERVES 6

1. Add the beef, beans, tomatoes, broth, enchilada sauce, onion, and garlic to a 4-quart slow cooker. Cover and cook on low 8 hours.
2. In a small bowl, whisk together the water and cornmeal; stir into the chili. Cover and cook on high an additional 15–30 minutes or until the chili is thickened.
3. Top each serving with the cilantro and cheese.

1 (1½-pound) boneless beef chuck roast, cut into bite-sized pieces
1 (15-ounce) can pinto or red kidney beans, rinsed and drained
1 (14.5-ounce) can diced tomatoes, undrained
1 (10.5-ounce) can condensed beef broth
1 (10-ounce) can enchilada sauce
1 large yellow onion, peeled and chopped
2 teaspoons bottled minced garlic
½ cup water
2½ tablespoons fine cornmeal
2 tablespoons chopped fresh cilantro
2 ounces queso blanco or Monterey jack cheese, shredded

Meatball and Vegetable Soup

SERVES 6-8

1. Add the broth, meatballs, beans, undrained tomatoes, and vegetables to a 4-quart Dutch oven over medium-high heat. Bring to a boil and stir in the pasta. Return to boiling; reduce heat and simmer uncovered about 10 minutes or until the pasta is cooked.
2. To serve, ladle the soup into bowls. If desired, serve sprinkled with Parmigiano-Reggiano.

3 (14-ounce) cans beef broth
1 (16-ounce) package frozen cooked meatballs, thawed
1 (15-ounce) can Great Northern or cannellini beans, rinsed and drained
1 (14.5-ounce) can diced tomatoes with Italian herbs, undrained
1 (10-ounce) package frozen mixed vegetables, thawed
1 cup dried small pasta, such as orzo
Freshly grated Parmigiano-Reggiano cheese to taste (optional)

Turkey Kielbasa Stew

SERVES 4-5

Place all the ingredients in a 4-quart slow cooker. Cover and cook on low 8–10 hours or on high 4–5 hours.

4 cups coarsely chopped green cabbage
4 medium russet potatoes, peeled and cubed
1 (1-pound) bag baby carrots
1 pound fully cooked turkey kielbasa, sliced
½ teaspoon dried basil, crushed
½ teaspoon dried thyme, crushed
Salt to taste
Freshly ground black pepper to taste
2 (14-ounce) cans reduced-sodium chicken broth

Sweet Potato Soup with Ginger

SERVES 6-8

1. Heat the oil in a deep 3½-quart nonstick skillet or large saucepan over medium heat. Add the celery and carrot; sauté 3–5 minutes or until soft. Add the onion and sauté until transparent. Add the garlic and ginger, and sauté an additional 30 seconds.

2. Pour 3 cups broth into the pan along with the potatoes. Bring to a boil; reduce heat, cover, and simmer 10 minutes or until the potatoes are cooked through. Periodically check the simmering pot to make sure it doesn't boil dry. Mash the potatoes with a fork or blend them with a stick blender.

3. Stir the remaining broth and cream into the soup. Bring to temperature. Add salt and pepper to taste. Stir in the sherry and garnish with chives if desired.

2 tablespoons extra-virgin olive oil
2 stalks celery, finely diced
1 large carrot, peeled and finely diced
1 large yellow onion, peeled and minced
1 clove garlic, minced
2 teaspoons grated fresh ginger
5 cups chicken broth, divided
4 medium sweet potatoes, peeled and diced
1 cup heavy cream
Salt to taste
Freshly ground black pepper to taste
¼ cup dry sherry (optional)
Chopped chives to taste (optional)

TAKING THE BLENDER TO THE POT

A stick blender is also sometimes referred to as an immersion blender or a hand blender. They're available in electric and cordless rechargeable-battery models. You can use them to purée soups with ease, and they're also excellent for making sauces. To clean, simply put the blades into some soapy water and run the appliance, then run in clear water.

Pho

SERVES 8-10

1. Trim the roast of any fat; cut the meat into 2" × 4" pieces and add them to a 4-quart slow cooker. Peel and quarter 2 of the onions. Cut the ginger into 1" pieces. Add the onion and ginger to the slow cooker along with the star anise, cloves, cinnamon stick, salt, broth, and enough water to cover the meat by about 1". Cook on low 6–8 hours or until the beef is pull-apart tender.

2. About 30 minutes before serving, peel the remaining onion; cut it into paper-thin slices and soak them in cold water. Cover the noodles with hot water and allow to soak 15–20 minutes or until softened and opaque white; drain in a colander.

3. Remove the meat from the broth with a slotted spoon; shred the meat. Strain the broth through a fine-mesh strainer, discarding the spices and onion; return the strained broth to the slow cooker along with the shredded meat. Set the slow cooker on high and bring the broth to a rolling boil. Stir the fish sauce and brown sugar into the broth.

4. Blanch the noodles in stages. Add ¼ of the noodles to a strainer and submerge in the boiling broth, being careful not to allow the slow cooker to boil over. The noodles will collapse and lose their stiffness in about 15–20 seconds. Pull the strainer from the broth, letting the excess broth drain back into cooker, and empty the noodles into bowls, allowing each serving to fill about ⅓ of the bowl. Ladle some of the hot broth and beef over each serving of noodles. Garnish with the onion slices, green onions, and chopped cilantro, and finish with freshly ground black pepper.

1 (3-pound) English-cut chuck roast
3 medium yellow onions, divided
4" piece ginger
5 star anise
6 whole cloves
1 (3") cinnamon stick
¼ teaspoon salt
2 cups beef broth
Water, as needed
1½–2 pounds small dried banh pho noodles
¼ cup fish sauce
1 tablespoon light brown sugar
3–4 green onions, green part only, cut into thin rings
⅓ cup chopped fresh cilantro
Freshly ground black pepper to taste

Persian Lentil and Rice Soup

SERVES 8-10

1. Add the oil to a 6-quart Dutch oven and bring to temperature over medium-high heat. Add the onion and sauté until transparent, about 5–7 minutes. Stir in the parsley and tomatoes; sauté 2–3 minutes and then add the broth, mint, lentils, and lemon juice. Bring to a boil; reduce heat, cover, and simmer 30 minutes.
2. Add the rice to a blender or food processor; pulse several times to break it into a coarse powder. Add the broken rice and bulgur to the Dutch oven; cover and simmer 75 minutes.
3. Stir in the remaining ingredients. Simmer until the soup is heated through.

2 tablespoons extra-virgin olive oil
1 large yellow onion, peeled and thinly sliced
1 tablespoon dried parsley
4 cups chopped tomatoes
10 cups chicken broth
2 teaspoons dried mint, crushed
1 cup lentils
1/8 cup fresh lemon juice
1/4 cup uncooked basmati rice
1/2 cup bulgur wheat, medium grind
2 tablespoons tomato paste
1/2 teaspoon granulated sugar
2 teaspoons sumac
2 teaspoons advieh (see recipe in sidebar)
Salt to taste
Freshly ground black pepper to taste

ADVIEH

To make this Persian seasoning mix, add 1 tablespoon edible dried rose petals, 1 tablespoon ground cinnamon, 1/4 teaspoon cardamom seeds, 1/4 teaspoon black peppercorns, 1/8 teaspoon turmeric, 1/2 teaspoon freshly ground nutmeg, 1/2 teaspoon cumin seeds, and 1/4 teaspoon coriander seeds to a blender or spice grinder; grind to a powder. Store in an airtight container.

Deluxe Potato Soup

SERVES 12

1. Rinse the chicken inside and out in cold, running water. Add the chicken to a large Dutch oven or stockpot along with the salt, pepper, quartered onion, smashed garlic, halved celery, and carrot pieces. Add enough water to cover the chicken. Bring to a simmer over medium heat; cover, lower the heat, and simmer 1 hour or until the chicken is cooked through.

2. Use tongs to move the chicken to a cutting board or platter; allow to sit until cool enough to handle. Remove and discard the bones and skin. Strain the broth, discarding the vegetables, and set aside.

3. Add the bacon to the Dutch oven or stockpot and cook it over medium heat until it begins to render some of its fat. Add the chopped celery, shredded carrot, and diced onion; sauté 5 minutes or until the onion is transparent and the celery is tender. Stir in the potatoes and baby carrots. Fry until potatoes just begin to brown, then stir in the cooked chicken, ham, and Canadian bacon.

4. Measure the reserved chicken broth and add enough water to bring it to 6 cups. Pour the broth into the pan; bring to a simmer. Lower heat, cover, and cook 5 minutes or until the potatoes and carrots are cooked through.

5. Add the cream cheese and Cheddar, stirring gently to melt the cheeses into the broth. Stir in the heavy cream and cook about 3 more minutes to bring the cream to temperature.

1 (3-pound) whole chicken
Salt to taste
Freshly ground black pepper to taste
1 large yellow onion, peeled and quartered
4 cloves garlic, smashed
2 stalks celery, cut in half
2 large carrots, peeled and cut in 1" pieces
Water, as needed
1 pound bacon, cut into small pieces
1 stalk celery, finely chopped
1 large carrot, peeled and shredded
1 small yellow or white onion, peeled and finely diced
8 large russet potatoes, peeled and diced
1 (1-pound) bag baby carrots, diced
1 (7-ounce) ham slice, diced
1 (7-ounce) package Canadian bacon, diced
1 (8-ounce) package cream cheese, cut into cubes
16 ounces medium Cheddar cheese, shredded
1 cup heavy cream

Italian Pasta and Bean Soup

SERVES 8-10

1. Add the beans and water to a 4-quart Dutch oven or stew pot and bring to a boil; cover, turn off heat, and let sit 1 hour. Drain the beans, discarding the water.

2. Return the beans to the pan along with all the other ingredients except the cooked pork (if using) and the pasta. Bring to a simmer over medium heat; reduce heat, cover, and simmer 1½–2 hours or until the beans are very tender. Remove the bay leaf and discard. Remove the ham hocks and set aside to cool.

3. Remove the meat from the ham hocks and cut it into bite-sized pieces. Add the ham hock meat along with the cooked pork (if using) and the pasta to the pan. Cover and cook 15 minutes, stirring occasionally, or until the pasta is tender.

2 cups dried cannellini or small white beans
6 cups water
2 pounds smoked ham hocks
1 bay leaf
2 cloves garlic, minced
1 small yellow onion, peeled and diced
1 (1-pound) bag baby carrots, cut into thirds
¼ cup chopped lovage or celery leaves
½ cup tomato sauce
Pinch dried red pepper flakes
¼ teaspoon dried oregano
Pinch dried rosemary
½ teaspoon dried basil
1 teaspoon dried parsley
½ teaspoon granulated sugar
6 cups water
1 cup chicken broth
Salt to taste
Freshly ground black pepper to taste
1 cup shredded cooked pork (optional)
1 cup dried small pasta, such as orzo or stars

Tortellini and Spinach Soup

SERVES 4-6

1. Add the oil to a large saucepan or Dutch oven; bring to temperature over medium heat. Add the onion and sauté 3 minutes or until transparent.
2. Stir in the broth, tomatoes, and spinach and bring to a boil. Stir in the tortellini; lower the heat, cover, and simmer for the amount of time suggested on the tortellini package. Serve topped with cheese if desired.

1 tablespoon extra-virgin olive oil
1 small yellow onion, peeled and finely chopped
2 (14-ounce) cans chicken broth
1 (15-ounce) can stewed Italian-style tomatoes, coarsely chopped
1 (13.5-ounce) can chopped spinach, drained
1 (16-ounce) package fresh or frozen tortellini
Freshly grated Parmigiano-Reggiano cheese to taste (optional)

Mock Turtle Soup

SERVES 8-10

1. Add the salt pork or bacon to a large Dutch oven and sauté it over medium heat long enough to render the fat. Add the celery and carrots and sauté 3–5 minutes or until tender. Add the onion and sauté until transparent. Add the garlic and sauté another 30 seconds. Melt the butter into the sautéed vegetables. Stir in the flour and cook until the roux turns the color of peanut butter, stirring constantly.

2. Gradually add the beef broth, whisking it in to mix thoroughly with the roux. Stir in the chicken broth and tomatoes. Stir in the basil, marjoram, thyme, bay leaf, pepper, and parsley. Bring to a boil, and boil 1 minute. Reduce heat and simmer until the mixture begins to thicken.

3. Add the halibut. Cover and simmer 10 minutes. Remove the halibut and flake it. Stir in the fish, beef, chicken, crabmeat, lemon juice, hot sauce, Worcestershire, and ground cloves. Reduce heat; simmer until the meat reaches serving temperature. Stir in the sherry and diced eggs. Serve hot.

¼ pound salt pork or bacon, diced
2 stalks celery, finely diced
2 large carrots, peeled and finely diced
1 medium yellow onion, peeled and diced
3 cloves garlic, minced
¼ cup butter
½ cup all-purpose flour
3 cups beef broth
1 cup chicken broth
1 (15-ounce) can diced tomatoes
½ teaspoon dried basil
½ teaspoon dried marjoram
½ teaspoon dried thyme
1 bay leaf
1 teaspoon freshly ground black pepper
1 tablespoon dried parsley
1 (4-ounce) halibut fillet
1 cup shredded cooked roast beef
1 cup shredded cooked chicken
½ cup shredded cooked crabmeat
2 tablespoons fresh lemon juice
¼ teaspoon hot sauce, or to taste
1½ tablespoons Worcestershire sauce
⅛ teaspoon ground cloves
½ cup dry sherry
4 large hard-boiled eggs, peeled and finely diced

Pork Steak and Cabbage Soup

SERVES 8-10

1. Add the oil to a 6-quart Dutch oven and bring to temperature over medium heat. Mince or shred 4 or 5 of the baby carrots and add them to the pan along with the celery; sauté 3–5 minutes or until soft. Add the onion and sauté until transparent, about 5 minutes. Add the garlic and sauté an additional 30 seconds.

2. Add the pork and potatoes to the Dutch oven and stir-fry 3–5 minutes or until the potatoes just begin to take on a golden brown color.

3. Deglaze the pan with some of the chicken broth, and then add the remaining broth. Bring the broth to a boil; reduce heat, cover, and simmer 45 minutes. Cut remaining carrots into 3 or 4 pieces each and add to the pan.

4. Add the cabbage in stages. Stir in ½ cup, cover the pan and allow to steam 5 minutes, stir cabbage into the soup, and then repeat until all the cabbage has been added. Add the juniper berries and wine or beer, if using. Cover and simmer 45 minutes, stirring occasionally. Add water if additional cooking liquid is needed. Serve topped with cheese if desired.

3 tablespoons extra-virgin olive oil
1 (1-pound) bag baby carrots, divided
2 stalks celery, finely diced
1 large yellow onion, peeled and diced
1 clove garlic, minced
2 pounds boneless pork steak, trimmed and diced
4 large russet or red potatoes, peeled or unpeeled, and diced
4 cups chicken broth
1 large head green cabbage, cored and shredded
1½ teaspoons juniper berries (optional)
½ cup dry white wine or beer (optional)
Shredded Cheddar cheese to taste (optional)

BEST OPTIONS

This hearty soup tastes even better after it's been refrigerated overnight and warmed up the next day. The traditional version doesn't have the extra carrot pieces in it; omit them if you wish. Serve the soup with pumpernickel or whole-grain bread and beer.

Scottish Broth

SERVES 6-8

1. Melt the butter over medium heat in a 6-quart Dutch oven or stockpot. Add the onion, celery, carrots, leeks, salt, and pepper; sauté 5 minutes or until the onion is transparent and the other vegetables are soft.
2. Cut away any excess fat from the lamb. Use a cleaver to cut the bones and meat into pieces. Add several pieces of the lamb and sauté until browned on all sides. Add the garlic and bay leaves; sauté 1 minute. Turn off the heat and remove the pan from the burner. Deglaze the pan with the Scotch or broth.
3. Add the remaining lamb, barley, cabbage, and turnip; pour in enough water to cover all the ingredients in the pan by 2". Return the pan to the burner and bring to a boil over medium-high heat; lower the heat to medium-low and simmer uncovered 2 hours or until thickened and the meat is tender. Periodically skim off any fat from the top.
4. Use tongs or a slotted spoon to remove the meat from the pot. When it's cool enough to handle, cut the meat away from the bone; discard the bones. Stir the meat into the broth along with the peas and parsley. Bring to temperature and ladle into bowls to serve.

¼ cup butter or extra-virgin olive oil
1 large yellow onion, peeled and diced
2 stalks celery, diced
3 large carrots, peeled and finely chopped
½ cup chopped leeks (white part only)
½ teaspoon salt
¼ teaspoon freshly ground black pepper
2 pounds lamb neck bones or lamb shanks
4 cloves garlic, minced
2 bay leaves
½ cup Scotch whisky or chicken broth
½ cup pearl barley, rinsed and drained
½ small head green cabbage, cored and shredded
1 cup peeled and diced turnip
Water, as needed
½ cup frozen peas
¼ cup minced fresh flat-leaf parsley

SCOTTISH BROTH OPTIONS

You can substitute 1 cup coleslaw mix for the shredded cabbage. For a richer soup, substitute chicken broth for some of the water. Add extra flavor by putting a few tablespoons of blue cheese into the bottom of each serving bowl before you ladle in the soup. The cheese will melt into the soup and give it a rich, hearty flavor.

Spanish Bean Soup

SERVES 12

1. Put the dried beans in an 8-quart stockpot or Dutch oven. Add enough water to cover the beans; cover and let soak overnight.
2. Drain the beans in a colander. Wipe out the pot and add the salt pork or bacon; cook over medium heat to render the fat. Add the chorizo, celery, and carrot; sauté 3–5 minutes or until soft. Add the onion and sauté until transparent, about 5 minutes. Add the garlic and sauté an additional 30 seconds.
3. Stir in the smoked ham. Add the beans and chicken. Stir in the broth, water, Worcestershire, and hot sauce. Bring to a simmer; cover and simmer 1 hour, stirring occasionally. Add more water if needed to keep the pot from boiling dry.
4. Remove the chicken and set aside. Stir the soup well and then stir in the potatoes and turnips. Add the cabbage and kale; cover and simmer 15 minutes.
5. Shred the chicken, discarding the skin and bones. Stir the shredded chicken into the soup. Add additional water, if needed. Bring to a simmer, cover, and simmer 45–60 minutes or until the beans are tender. Add salt and pepper to taste.

½ pound dried white beans
Water, as needed to soak beans
¼ pound salt pork or bacon, diced
½ pound Spanish chorizo, diced or thinly sliced
1 stalk celery, finely chopped
1 large carrot, peeled and shredded
1 large yellow onion, peeled and diced
3 cloves garlic, minced
½ pound smoked ham, diced
4 bone-on, skin-on chicken thighs
1 cup chicken, pork, or ham broth
4 cups water
2 teaspoons Worcestershire sauce
Hot sauce to taste
4 large russet potatoes, peeled and diced
4 turnips, peeled, quartered, and sliced
1 small head green cabbage, cored and shredded
2 cups thinly sliced kale (tough stems removed)
Salt to taste
Freshly ground black pepper to taste

Porcini Mushroom and Barley Soup

SERVES 8-10

1. Put the dried mushrooms in a small bowl and pour the 1 cup warm water over them. Set aside to soak 30 minutes.
2. Add the 2 cups water to a 6-quart Dutch oven or stockpot and bring to a boil over medium-high heat. Stir in the barley; reduce heat, cover, and simmer 15 minutes or until all liquid is absorbed. Stir in the butter.
3. Use a slotted spoon to remove the mushrooms from the soaking liquid; dice about half of the mushrooms and then stir all the mushrooms into the barley mixture.
4. Add the broth, carrots, potatoes, celery, green beans, and parsley. Stir well to separate the grains of barley. Bring to a simmer, cover, and cook 1 hour or until the barley is tender. Season with salt and pepper to taste. Ladle the soup into bowls and top each serving with a dollop of sour cream if desired.

1 ounce dried porcini or oyster mushrooms
1 cup warm water
2 cups water
1 cup pearl barley
¼ cup butter
8–10 cups beef broth
2 large carrots, peeled and diced
2 large russet potatoes, peeled and diced
1 stalk celery, diced
1 (10-ounce) package cut frozen green beans, thawed
1 teaspoon dried parsley
Salt to taste
Freshly ground black pepper to taste
Sour cream to taste (optional)

STRETCHING THE SOUP

To stretch this recipe to 10 servings instead of 8, use all 10 cups of beef broth. Either way, the final result will be a rich soup that, when served along with a salad and a dinner roll or toasted whole-grain bread, is a worthy main course. Or, if you prefer, you can use the mushroom soaking liquid in place of some of the broth; just strain it first to remove any grit or sand from the mushrooms.

Tuscan Bean Soup

SERVES 8-10

1. Rinse the beans and add them to a 6-quart Dutch oven along with 6 cups water. Bring to a boil; reduce heat and simmer uncovered 2 minutes. Remove from heat, cover, and let stand 1 hour. Drain the beans in a colander; set aside.

2. Wipe out the pan. Add the oil and bring to temperature over medium heat. Add the celery and carrot; sauté 3–5 minutes or until soft. Add the onion and sauté until transparent, about 5 minutes. Add the garlic and sauté an additional 30 seconds.

3. Add the beef and cook about 5 minutes or until browned. Add the drained beans and remaining 4 cups water, the beef broth, ham hocks, bay leaf, thyme, rosemary, pepper, and salt; bring to a boil. Reduce heat, cover, and simmer 1½ hours, stirring occasionally and adding more water if necessary.

4. Remove the bay leaf, ham hocks, and beef; set aside to cool. Remove the meat from the bones, cut into bite-sized pieces, and stir into the soup. Discard the bones and bay leaf. Cover and simmer 30 minutes or until the beans and meats are tender. Skim off any fat from the surface of the soup. Stir in the spinach. Heat through and serve.

8 ounces dry white kidney, cannellini, or Great Northern beans
10 cups water (or more as needed), divided
1 tablespoon extra-virgin olive oil
2 stalks celery, diced
3 large carrots, peeled and diced
3 medium yellow onions, peeled and diced
4 cloves garlic, minced
1 pound crosscut beef shanks, 1–1½" thick
1 (14-ounce) can reduced-sodium beef broth
4 smoked ham hocks
1 bay leaf
½ teaspoon dried thyme, crushed
½ teaspoon dried rosemary, crushed
¼ teaspoon freshly ground black pepper
Salt to taste
4 cups torn fresh spinach leaves

Chicken Chili

SERVES 4

1. Add oil to a pressure cooker and bring it to temperature over medium heat. Add the chicken and stir-fry 5 minutes. Add the jalapeño and red pepper; stir-fry with chicken 2 minutes. Stir in the onion; sauté 3 minutes or until tender. Stir in the garlic, tomatoes, kidney beans, paprika, tomato paste, broth, thyme, oregano, chili powder, salt, and pepper.
2. Lock the lid in place. Bring to low pressure, lower the heat, and maintain pressure 10 minutes. Remove the pan from the burner and use the quick-release method to release the pressure.

2 tablespoons vegetable oil

2 pounds boneless, skinless chicken thighs, cut into bite-sized cubes

1 medium jalapeño pepper, seeded and minced

1 small red bell pepper, seeded and diced

1 small yellow onion, peeled and diced

1 clove garlic, minced

1 (15-ounce) can diced tomatoes

1 (16-ounce) can red kidney beans, rinsed and drained

1 tablespoon paprika

1 tablespoon tomato paste

1 cup chicken broth

¼ teaspoon dried thyme

¼ teaspoon dried oregano

1 teaspoon chili powder

Salt to taste

Freshly ground black pepper to taste

Shrimp and Crab Bisque

SERVES 6-8

1. Melt 2 tablespoons butter in a 6-quart Dutch oven or stockpot over medium heat. Add the celery and stir into the butter. Finely dice the baby carrots and stir them into the butter and celery; sauté 2 minutes. Add the onion and sauté until transparent. Stir in the garlic.
2. Add the stock or broth and the potatoes to the pot.
3. Wrap the cloves, bay leaf, and peppercorns in cheesecloth or put them in a muslin cooking bag; add to the broth. Bring to a boil; lower the temperature, cover, and simmer 10 minutes.
4. Add the milk. Bring to a boil over medium heat. Mix ½ cup butter and flour together to form a paste and stir it into the broth, 1 teaspoon at a time. Once all the butter-flour mixture is added, boil 1 minute, then lower the temperature and let simmer until the mixture begins to thicken and the raw flour taste is cooked out of the broth. Remove the cheesecloth or cooking bag.
5. Add the shrimp and cook just until they begin to turn pink; do not overcook. Stir in the crabmeat and cream. Bring to temperature. If desired, season with salt, white pepper, and/or dry sherry. Remove from heat and serve immediately. Garnish with parsley or green onion if desired.

2 tablespoons plus ½ cup butter, divided
4 stalks celery with leaves, finely chopped
6 baby carrots
1 large yellow onion, peeled and finely chopped
2 cloves garlic, minced
3 cups fish or shrimp stock, or chicken broth
4 large russet potatoes, peeled and diced
2 whole cloves
1 bay leaf
6 peppercorns
2 cups whole milk
½ cup all-purpose flour
1 pound raw shrimp, peeled and deveined
1 pound cooked crabmeat, broken apart
2 cups heavy cream
Salt to taste (optional)
White pepper to taste (optional)
Dry sherry to taste (optional)
Chopped fresh flat-leaf parsley or green onions (green part only) to taste (optional)

Slow Cooker Texas Chili

SERVES 6-8

1. Add all the ingredients to a 4-quart slow cooker and stir to combine. The liquid in your slow cooker should completely cover the meat and vegetables. If additional liquid is needed, add more crushed tomatoes, broth, or water.
2. Cook on low 6–8 hours.

¼ pound bacon, diced
1 stalk celery, finely chopped
1 large carrot, peeled and finely chopped
1 (2-pound) chuck roast, cubed
2 large yellow onions, peeled and diced
6 cloves garlic, diced
6 medium jalapeño peppers, seeded and diced
Salt to taste
Freshly ground black pepper to taste
¼ cup chili powder
1 teaspoon Mexican oregano
1 teaspoon ground cumin
1 teaspoon light brown sugar (optional)
1 (28-ounce) can diced tomatoes
1 cup beef broth

Ground Lamb and Bean Chili

SERVES 6-8

1. Add the lamb, oil, onion, garlic, chili powder, and cumin seeds to a large Dutch oven over medium heat. Sauté until the meat is brown and the onion is transparent, about 10 minutes.
2. Add remaining ingredients. Add water, if needed, so that all the ingredients are covered by liquid. Continue to cook on medium about 15 minutes to bring all the ingredients to temperature, then lower the heat, cover, and simmer 1½ hours. Check the pot periodically to stir the chili and to make sure that it doesn't boil dry. Add more water, if necessary.

2 pounds ground lamb
3 tablespoons extra-virgin olive oil
1 large yellow onion, peeled and diced
4 cloves garlic, crushed
2 tablespoons chili powder
1 tablespoon whole cumin seeds
¼ teaspoon dried oregano, crushed
2 medium jalapeño peppers, seeded and diced
2 medium green bell peppers, seeded and diced
1 (28-ounce) can diced tomatoes
1 (8-ounce) can tomato sauce
1 tablespoon Worcestershire sauce
2 (15-ounce) cans red kidney beans, rinsed and drained
Salt to taste
Freshly ground black pepper to taste
Water, as needed

MAKE YOUR OWN CHILI POWDER

To make your own chili powder: Add 5 dried poblano peppers, 1 dried ancho chili pepper, ⅜ teaspoon ground cumin, ¾ teaspoon dried oregano, and 1 teaspoon garlic powder to a spice grinder, food processor, or blender. Process until fine. Add cayenne pepper to taste. Store in the freezer in a tightly covered container and it'll keep indefinitely.

Chipotle Chili

SERVES 4

1. Add the ground beef and chili powder to a deep 3½-quart nonstick skillet; brown the meat over medium-high heat, breaking it apart as it cooks. When the meat is almost cooked through, add the onion; lower heat to medium and sauté the onion until transparent, about 5 more minutes. Drain off any excess fat.
2. Add the garlic and sauté 30 seconds. Stir in the kidney beans, salsa, corn, and broth. Bring to temperature and simmer 15 minutes. Add salt and pepper to taste.

1 pound lean ground beef
1 tablespoon chili powder
1 medium yellow onion, peeled and diced
2 cloves garlic, minced
1 (15-ounce) can red kidney beans, rinsed and drained
1 cup chipotle salsa
1 cup frozen whole-kernel corn
1 (14-ounce) can beef broth
Salt to taste
Freshly ground black pepper to taste

Quick and Easy Beef Stew

SERVES 4

1. Add the roast beef, soups, Worcestershire, water, and vegetables to a 6-quart Dutch oven. Bring to a boil over high heat. Lower heat, cover, and simmer 6 minutes.
2. In a small bowl, mix the butter into the flour to make a paste. Ladle about ½ cup of the broth into the bowl and whisk into the paste, then pour it into the stew. Increase heat to medium-high and return to a boil; boil 2 minutes, stirring occasionally.
3. Reduce heat, cover, and simmer an additional 2 minutes or until the vegetables are tender and the stew is thickened. Add salt and pepper to taste.

1 pound cooked roast beef, cut into bite-sized pieces
1 (10¾-ounce) can condensed tomato soup
1 (10¾-ounce) can condensed French onion soup
1 tablespoon Worcestershire sauce
2 cups water
4 cups frozen vegetables of your choice
1 tablespoon butter
1 tablespoon all-purpose flour
Salt to taste
Freshly ground black pepper to taste

Seafood Stew

SERVES 8

1. Bring the oil to temperature in a 4–6-quart Dutch oven over medium heat. Add the onions, garlic, and sausage; stirring frequently, sauté 5 minutes or until the onions are transparent.
2. Add the thyme, oregano, bay leaf, and potatoes, stirring everything to mix the herbs and coat the potatoes in the oil. Pour in the broth; bring to a simmer. Add the kale; cover and simmer 10 minutes or until the potatoes are nearly tender.
3. Add the fish; cook 3 minutes. Add water if additional liquid is needed to cover the fish. Add the drained clams and cook an additional 3 minutes or until the fish is cooked and the clams are brought to temperature.
4. Add salt and pepper to taste. Garnish with chopped parsley if desired, and drizzle with extra-virgin olive oil.

2 tablespoons extra-virgin olive oil, plus extra for serving
2 medium yellow onions, peeled and diced
4 cloves garlic, minced
1 pound smoked sausage, sliced into chunks
½ teaspoon dried thyme
¼ teaspoon dried oregano, crushed
1 bay leaf
8 large Yukon gold potatoes, diced
8 cups chicken broth
1 pound kale, chopped
Water, as needed (optional)
2 pounds perch, cod, or bass fillets, skin and pin bones removed
2 (28-ounce) cans boiled baby clams, drained
Sea salt to taste
Freshly ground black pepper to taste
¼ cup chopped fresh flat-leaf parsley (optional)

WHY WATER IS OPTIONAL

The heat at which you cook a dish makes a difference in how much of the liquid will evaporate during the cooking process. Some vegetables in a dish also sometimes absorb more liquid than do others. If such evaporation or absorption occurs, the broth will become concentrated. Thus, water only reintroduces more liquid; it doesn't dilute the taste.

African Peanut and Chicken Stew

SERVES 6

1. Add the oil to a 6-quart Dutch oven and bring it to temperature over medium heat. Add the chicken pieces, skin-side down, and brown. Add the onion, dill, bay leaves, and enough water to almost cover the chicken; bring to a boil. Reduce heat, cover, and simmer 45 minutes.
2. Remove the chicken from the pot and keep warm; discard the skin, if desired. Remove and discard the bay leaves.
3. Add ½ cup of the hot liquid from the Dutch oven to the peanut butter; mix well, and then pour the resulting peanut butter sauce into the pan.
4. In a small bowl, mix together the cornstarch and cold water; remove any lumps. Whisk the cornstarch mixture into the broth in the pan, continuing to stir or whisk until the broth thickens. If you prefer a thicker sauce, mix more cornstarch in cold water and repeat the process.
5. Add salt and pepper to taste. The traditional way to serve this dish is to place the chicken over some cooked rice. Ladle the thickened pan juices over the chicken and rice. Top with fried bananas, pineapple, and toasted coconut, and chopped peanuts if desired.

2 tablespoons peanut oil
2 (3-pound) chickens, cut into serving pieces
1 large yellow onion, peeled and sliced
½ teaspoon dried dill
2 bay leaves
Water, as needed
½ cup peanut butter
3 tablespoons cornstarch
½ cup cold water
Salt to taste
Freshly ground black pepper to taste
3–6 cups cooked long-grain rice (optional)
5 medium bananas, peeled and cut lengthwise, then browned in butter (optional)
Unsweetened pineapple chunks (optional)
4 ounces unsweetened shredded coconut, toasted (optional)
½ cup finely chopped roasted peanuts

TOASTING COCONUT

If you would like to add the toasted coconut to this recipe it is very easy to make. First, preheat oven to 350°F. Spread the coconut out over a sheet pan or cookie sheet. Place the pan in the oven and, watching it carefully, bake 5 minutes or until the coconut is a very light golden brown.

Green Chili Stew

SERVES 6-8

1. Melt the butter in a 4-quart Dutch oven over medium heat. Add the onion and sauté 5 minutes or until transparent.
2. Stir in the oregano, garlic, and chili powder. Whisk in the flour to make a roux, and cook until lightly browned, about 5 minutes.
3. Whisk in the broth a little at a time, whisking until smooth. Bring to a boil and boil 1 minute. Reduce heat and stir in the pork and chilies. Simmer gently, stirring occasionally, until thickened. Add salt and pepper to taste.

½ cup butter
1 large yellow onion, peeled and diced
½ teaspoon dried oregano
½ tablespoon granulated garlic
1 tablespoon chili powder
¼ cup all-purpose flour
4 cups chicken broth
1 (28-ounce) can heat-and-serve pork
3 (7-ounce) cans mild or hot green chilies, drained and chopped
Salt to taste
Freshly ground black pepper to taste

Spiced Armenian Lamb Stew

SERVES 4-6

1. Melt the butter in a 6-quart Dutch oven and bring to temperature over medium heat. Add the onions and sauté 3 minutes.
2. Push the onions to the side of the pan, add the lamb, and brown the meat in the butter. Stir the paprika, pepper, allspice, and cinnamon into the meat and onions. Add salt to taste.
3. Push the meat and onions to the side and sauté the tomato paste 2 minutes, then stir it into the meat and onions. Slowly pour the water into the pan. Stir to dissolve the tomato paste into the water. Bring to a boil, then reduce heat, cover, and simmer 45 minutes or until the meat is tender.
4. Add the red wine, cover, and simmer 15 more minutes.

2 tablespoons butter
1 large yellow onion, peeled and diced
2 pounds lean, boneless leg of lamb, cut into 1" cubes
½ teaspoon paprika
½ teaspoon freshly ground black pepper
½ teaspoon ground allspice
¼ teaspoon ground cinnamon
Salt to taste
¼ cup tomato paste
1 cup water
2 tablespoons dry red wine

Irish Lamb Stew

SERVES 6-8

1. Bring the oil or fat to temperature over medium heat in a large Dutch oven. Add the yellow onion and sauté 3–5 minutes or until transparent. Add the garlic and sauté an additional 30 seconds.

2. Add the lamb; brown it about 5 minutes or until it begins to release some of its juices and some of the pieces become caramelized.

3. Sprinkle the flour over the lamb and stir to toss the flour with the meat and fat in the pan. Stir in the broth, salt, pepper, bay leaf, marjoram, and lemon juice. Bring to a simmer, cover, and simmer 30–60 minutes or until the meat begins to get tender. If needed, skim off any excess fat from the top of the broth.

4. Add the mushrooms, carrots, and potatoes; cover and simmer 30 minutes or until the carrots and potatoes are cooked through. Serve sprinkled with parsley if desired.

¼ cup extra-virgin olive oil or bacon fat
1 large yellow onion, peeled and chopped
1 clove garlic, minced
2½ pounds lean lamb shoulder, cut in bite-sized pieces
2 tablespoons all-purpose flour
1½ cups chicken broth
Salt to taste
¼ teaspoon freshly ground black pepper
1 bay leaf
¼ teaspoon dried marjoram
2 teaspoons lemon juice
1 cup sliced mushrooms
4 large carrots, peeled and cut into chunks
4 large russet potatoes, peeled and diced
1½ tablespoons finely chopped fresh parsley (optional)

Puerto Rican Chicken Stew

SERVES 4

1. Add the oregano, black pepper, paprika, and salt to a large resealable plastic bag; shake to mix the spices. Add the chicken and shake to coat the chicken in the spices.
2. Add the olive oil to a large Dutch oven and bring to temperature over medium heat. Add the salt pork or bacon, onion, and green pepper. Sauté 3–5 minutes or until the onion is transparent and the green pepper begins to get tender.
3. Stir in the ham and tomato; reduce heat to low, cover, and simmer 10 minutes. Stir in the chorizo or smoked sausage, and then add the chicken, skin-side down, with as many of the chicken pieces touching the pan bottom as possible. Cover and simmer 30 minutes.
4. Add the olives, capers, Annatto Oil, rice, and water; bring to a simmer, cover, and simmer 15 minutes. Add the peas; cover and simmer another 5 minutes or until the chicken is cooked through and the rice is tender.

2 teaspoons dried oregano, crushed
$1/4$ teaspoon freshly ground black pepper
2 teaspoons paprika
$1/4$ teaspoon salt
1 ($3\frac{1}{2}$-pound) chicken, cut into serving pieces
$1/4$ cup extra-virgin olive oil
1 ounce salt pork or bacon, diced
1 medium yellow onion, peeled and diced
1 medium green bell pepper, seeded and diced
2 ounces ham, diced
1 medium tomato, diced
$1/2$ pound chorizo or smoked sausage
$1/4$ cup small pimiento-stuffed olives
1 tablespoon capers, rinsed and drained
1 tablespoon Annatto Oil (see sidebar)
2 cups converted rice
3 cups water
$1/2$ cup frozen peas

ANNATTO OIL

To make Annatto Oil, put $1/2$ cup peanut, sesame, or vegetable oil in a small, heavy saucepan and heat until the oil smokes, or reaches about 350°F. Remove the pan from the heat and stir $1/4$ cup annatto seeds into the oil. Cool and strain the seeds from the oil. Store in a covered jar in the refrigerator.

Simplified Bouillabaisse

SERVES 8

1. Add the oil to a Dutch oven and bring to temperature over medium heat. Add the yellow and green onions; sauté 5 minutes or until transparent. Add the garlic and sauté another 30 seconds.

2. Add the tomato juice or broth, tomatoes, wine, water, bay leaf, pepper, tarragon, thyme, and parsley; bring to a boil. Reduce heat, cover, and simmer 1 hour. Remove the bay leaf. At this point, this broth can be refrigerated and reheated later to finish the dish.

3. Add the fish pieces; simmer 10 minutes or until the fish is opaque and cooked through. Stir in the shrimp, clams, and mussels; simmer 2–3 minutes to bring all the ingredients to temperature. Serve with toasted garlic toast if desired.

⅓ cup extra-virgin olive oil
1 large yellow onion, peeled and sliced
1 bunch green onions (4–5 stalks), sliced
1 clove garlic, minced
2 cups tomato juice or chicken broth
1 (14.5-ounce) can diced tomatoes
1 cup Chardonnay or other dry white wine
2 cups water
1 bay leaf
½ teaspoon freshly ground black pepper
1 teaspoon dried tarragon, crumbled
½ teaspoon thyme, crushed
1 tablespoon parsley, crushed
1 pound whitefish, cut into 1" pieces
1 pound frozen cooked shrimp, thawed
2 (3.53-ounce) pouches whole baby clams
1 (10-ounce) can boiled mussels, drained
Garlic toast (optional)

THE PERFECT GARLIC TOAST

To make delicious garlic toast simply preheat the oven to 400°F. Slice French bread into ¼"-thick slices. Brush both sides of the bread with extra-virgin olive oil, place flat on a baking sheet, and bake 10 minutes or until crisp and lightly browned. While the toast is still warm, rub a cut clove of garlic over the top of each slice. Allow 2 slices per serving.

French Veal Stew

SERVES 6-8

1. Add the veal and veal bones to a 4-quart Dutch oven. Add enough cold water to cover the meat; bring to a boil over high heat. Reduce heat and simmer 3 minutes or until a heavy scum rises to the top of the pan. Drain the meat and bones in a colander and rinse to remove the scum; set aside.

2. Wipe out the Dutch oven. Melt 2 tablespoons butter over medium heat. Add the carrot and celery; sauté 5 minutes or until tender. Add the veal and veal bones along with the broth, onion, parsley, bay leaf, and thyme. If needed, add enough water to bring the liquid level up to the top of the meat. Bring to a boil; reduce heat, cover, and simmer 1½ hours or until the veal is tender.

3. Skim any scum from the surface and discard. Add salt to taste. Let the meat rest in the broth uncovered 30 minutes. Pour the contents of the pan into a colander set over a large bowl to hold the broth.

4. Melt 2 tablespoons butter in the Dutch oven over medium heat. Add the mushrooms and sauté 5 minutes, stirring occasionally. Return the broth to the pan, adding water if necessary to bring the broth to 4 cups.

4 pounds veal stew meat, cut into 2" pieces
1 pound veal bones, sawed into pieces
Water, as needed
8 tablespoons butter, divided
1 large carrot, peeled and finely diced
1 stalk celery, finely diced
2½ cups veal or chicken broth
1 large white onion, peeled and studded with 1 whole clove
1 tablespoon dried parsley
½ bay leaf
Pinch dried thyme, crushed
Salt to taste
8 ounces button or cremini mushrooms, sliced
5 tablespoons all-purpose flour
1 tablespoon lemon juice
1 (1-pound) bag frozen pearl onions, thawed
3 large egg yolks
½ cup heavy cream
Gremolata to taste (optional)

5. Melt the remaining 4 tablespoons butter in a small microwave-safe bowl. Whisk in the flour and lemon juice. Once the broth begins to boil, whisk in the flour mixture, stirring constantly for 2 minutes or until the broth begins to thicken. Stir in the pearl onions. Reduce heat and simmer uncovered while you prepare the final touches.

6. Discard the onion and veal bones. Add the veal meat to the Dutch oven. In a small bowl, whisk the egg yolks together with the cream. Slowly whisk in a cup of the thickened broth from the pan to temper the eggs. Remove the pan from the heat, then slowly whisk the egg mixture into the remaining thickened broth in the pan. Set the pan back over low heat and stir gently to allow the egg yolks to cook into the sauce, being careful not to allow the sauce to return to a simmer.

7. If desired, stir some of the gremolata into the stew before you garnish each serving with it.

GREMOLATA

Gremolata is a garlic-citrus condiment for stews. Remove the zest from an orange and a lemon; blanch in 4 cups water for 10 minutes. Drain and rinse in cold water. Pat dry, then finely chop it along with 1 clove garlic and 1/4 cup chopped fresh flat-leaf parsley. Sprinkle over the stew, to taste.

Lobster Chowder

SERVES 4

1. Add the bacon to a 4-quart Dutch oven and fry it over medium heat until golden and nearly crisp. If the bacon renders more than 2 tablespoons of fat, pour off the excess. Add the leeks, stir to coat them in the bacon fat, and sauté 2 minutes.
2. Stir in the potatoes and reduce heat to low; cover and cook 10 minutes or until the potatoes are tender, stirring frequently to prevent browning. Mash some of the potatoes with a fork if desired. Add the water, stock, or broth; bring to a simmer, cover, and cook 5 minutes.
3. Whisk the butter into the broth. Once the butter is melted, add the pepper, lobster, and cream. Stir gently and cook on low to bring all the ingredients to temperature. Add salt, additional black pepper, and cayenne or hot sauce if desired.
4. Remove the pan from the stove, cover, and allow the chowder to ripen 15–20 minutes before serving. Ladle into warmed shallow soup bowls; sprinkle with parsley if desired.

2 ounces smoked slab bacon, cut into ¼" dice
2 medium leeks (white part only), cut into ½" dice
4 medium russet or red potatoes, peeled and diced
4 cups water, lobster or fish stock, or chicken broth
2 tablespoons unsalted butter
Freshly ground black pepper to taste
1 pound cooked lobster, cut into bite-sized pieces
1 cup heavy cream
Sea salt to taste
Pinch cayenne pepper or dash hot sauce (optional)
Chopped fresh parsley (optional)

HEALTHIER ALTERNATIVE

If you don't want to use heavy cream in this recipe, decrease the amount of water, stock, or broth by a cup and add 2 cups of milk. Do not use half-and-half because it has a tendency to curdle.

Marsala Beef Stew

1. Add the oil and butter to a 4-quart Dutch oven over medium-high heat. Add 10 pieces of the beef to the pan and cook 5 minutes or until the meat takes on a dark outer color.
2. Reduce heat to medium and add the carrot and celery; sauté 3–5 minutes or until soft. Add the onion and sauté until transparent, about 5 minutes. Add the garlic and sauté an additional 30 seconds. Stir in the mushrooms; sauté until tender.
3. Add the remaining meat, the wines, rosemary, oregano, and basil. Add water, if needed, to bring the liquid level to just over the top of the meat. Reduce heat, cover, and simmer 1½ hours or until the meat is tender.
4. Taste the broth. Simmer uncovered long enough to reduce the broth if it tastes weak. Add salt and pepper if needed. Remove from heat and let rest uncovered 30 minutes.
5. Place the pan over low heat to bring the stew back to temperature.

2 tablespoons extra-virgin olive oil
1 tablespoon butter or ghee
3 pounds English-cut chuck roast, cut into bite-sized pieces
1 large carrot, peeled and finely diced
1 stalk celery, finely diced
1 large yellow onion, peeled and diced
3 cloves garlic, minced
8 ounces button or cremini mushrooms, sliced
½ cup dry white wine
1 cup Marsala wine
½ teaspoon dried rosemary
½ teaspoon dried oregano
½ teaspoon dried basil
Water, as needed
Salt to taste
Freshly ground black pepper to taste

SEARING MEAT

Searing meat does not seal in the juices, but it does intensify the flavor of a dish by adding another flavor dimension. Therefore, while it isn't necessary to sear all the meat, it is a good idea to do so with some of it before you add the liquid and begin to simmer a stew.

Sweet and Hot Chili

SERVES 8-10

1. Add the ground chuck, pork, onion, garlic, cumin seeds, chili powder, and oregano to a large Dutch oven; cook over medium heat until the beef and pork are browned and cooked through. Drain off any excess fat and discard.
2. Stir in the tomatoes, ketchup, cinnamon, cloves, brown sugar, kidney beans, beef broth, and Worcestershire (if using). Bring to a simmer; reduce heat, cover, and simmer 1 hour. Stir the chili occasionally, and add water if needed.
3. Add salt, pepper, and hot sauce to taste if desired. You may also wish to add more brown sugar or chili powder according to your taste.

1 pound ground chuck
1 pound ground pork
2 large yellow onions, diced
6 cloves garlic, minced
1 teaspoon whole cumin seeds
2 tablespoons chili powder
¼ teaspoon dried oregano
1 (28-ounce) can diced tomatoes
¼ cup ketchup
¼ teaspoon ground cinnamon
¼ teaspoon ground cloves
2 tablespoons light brown sugar
2 (15-ounce) cans kidney beans, rinsed and drained
1 (14-ounce) can reduced-sodium beef broth
1 tablespoon Worcestershire sauce (optional)
Water, if needed
Salt to taste
Freshly ground black pepper to taste
Hot sauce to taste (optional)

TRY IT IN THE SLOW COOKER

If you want to make this chili in a slow cooker, follow step 1, and then add the cooked meat mixture, tomatoes, ketchup, cinnamon, cloves, brown sugar, kidney beans, beef broth, and Worcestershire (if using) to the slow cooker. Add water if needed to bring the liquid level to the top of the beans and meat. Cook on low 6–8 hours.

Tex-Mex Beef Stew

SERVES 8

1. Add the oil to a pressure cooker and bring it to temperature over medium-high heat. Add the beef and stir-fry 8 minutes or until well browned.

2. Stir in the chilies, tomatoes, tomato sauce, onion, bell pepper, garlic, cumin, black pepper, cayenne, lime juice, and jalapeños. If needed, add enough broth or water so that all the ingredients in the cooker are covered by liquid. Lock the lid, lower the heat to medium, and bring to high pressure; maintain 45 minutes.

3. Let the pan remain on the burner and allow 15 minutes or more for the pressure to drop on its own. Remove the lid and stir in the cilantro. Serve immediately.

2 tablespoons extra-virgin olive or vegetable oil
1 (4-pound) English or chuck roast, trimmed of fat and cut into 1" cubes
1 (7-ounce) can green chilies
2 (15-ounce) cans diced tomatoes
1 (8-ounce) can tomato sauce
1 large sweet onion, peeled and diced
1 medium green bell pepper, seeded and diced
6 cloves garlic, minced
1 tablespoon ground cumin
1 teaspoon freshly ground black pepper
Cayenne pepper to taste
2 tablespoons lime juice
2 medium jalapeño peppers, seeded and diced
Beef broth or water, as needed
1 bunch fresh cilantro, chopped

Southern Chicken Stew

SERVES 8

1. Bring the bacon fat to temperature in a 6-quart Dutch oven over medium heat. Add the chicken pieces and fry until lightly browned.
2. Add the water, tomatoes, onions, sugar, and wine or apple juice. Bring to a simmer; cover and simmer 75 minutes or until the chicken is cooked through. Use a slotted spoon to remove the chicken and set it aside until it's cool enough to handle. Remove the chicken from the bones and discard the skin and bones. Shred the chicken meat and set aside.
3. Add the lima beans, corn, and okra to the pot. Bring to a simmer and cook uncovered 30 minutes.
4. Stir in the shredded chicken, bread crumbs, and Worcestershire. Simmer 10 minutes, stirring occasionally, to bring the chicken to temperature and thicken the stew. Add salt, pepper, and hot sauce if desired.

3 tablespoons bacon fat
1 (3-pound) chicken, cut into serving pieces
2 cups water
1 (28-ounce) can diced tomatoes
2 large yellow onions, peeled and sliced
½ teaspoon granulated sugar
½ cup dry white wine or apple juice
1 (10-ounce) package frozen lima beans, thawed
1 (10-ounce) package frozen whole-kernel corn, thawed
1 (10-ounce) package frozen okra, thawed and sliced
1 cup bread crumbs, toasted
3 tablespoons Worcestershire sauce
Salt to taste
Freshly ground black pepper to taste
Hot sauce to taste (optional)

Unstuffed Tomatoes and Peppers

SERVES 8

1. In a large mixing bowl, combine the rice, tomato juice, beef, lamb or pork, onion, parsley, salt, black pepper, paprika, allspice, cinnamon, and sugar. Set aside.
2. Add 1 can diced tomatoes to a 4-quart or larger slow cooker. Add half of the meat-rice mixture. Spread the diced green peppers over the top of the meat mixture, and top the peppers with the rest of the meat. Add the remaining can tomatoes, broth, and lemon juice. If needed, add additional water or broth to bring the liquid to almost the top of the solid ingredients.
3. Cook 6–8 hours on low. If too much liquid remains in the slow cooker, cook uncovered long enough to allow some of the liquid to evaporate.

1 cup uncooked long-grain rice
1 cup tomato juice
1 pound ground beef
½ pound ground lamb or pork
1 large yellow onion, peeled and diced
1 tablespoon dried parsley
1 teaspoon salt
Freshly ground black pepper to taste
1 teaspoon paprika
⅛ teaspoon ground allspice
Pinch ground cinnamon
1 teaspoon granulated sugar
2 (14.5-ounce) cans diced tomatoes
4 medium green bell peppers, seeded and diced
1 cup beef broth
2 tablespoons lemon juice
Water or additional broth, as needed

Romanian Veal with Vegetables Stew

SERVES 8

1. Add the flour, salt, and pepper to a large food-storage bag; shake to mix. Add the veal cubes and toss to coat in the seasoned flour.
2. Melt the butter in an ovenproof 6-quart Dutch oven over medium heat. Add the veal and brown 5 minutes. Add the onions and sauté, stirring frequently, 5 minutes or until transparent. Add the garlic and sauté an additional 30 seconds.
3. Preheat oven to 350°F.
4. Add the broth, wine, and half of the cabbage to the Dutch oven; cover and simmer until the cabbage wilts, then add all the remaining ingredients. Bring to a boil, cover, and bake 1 hour, stirring the stew about every 20 minutes. The stew is done when the meat and all the vegetables are cooked through and tender.

3 tablespoons all-purpose flour
½ teaspoon salt
¼ teaspoon freshly ground black pepper
1 pound boneless veal shoulder, cut into 1" cubes
2 tablespoons butter
1 medium yellow onion, peeled and sliced
2 small cloves garlic, minced
½ cup beef broth
½ cup dry red wine
1 small head green cabbage, cored and thinly sliced
2 teaspoons dried parsley
1 tablespoon tomato paste
2 large carrots, peeled and sliced
1 (14.5-ounce) can diced tomatoes
1 large green bell pepper, seeded and cut into strips
2 cups diced eggplant
2 cups diced zucchini
1 cup thinly sliced leeks (white part only)
2 small turnips, peeled and diced
1 cup diced celery root
2 small parsnips, peeled and diced
1 (14.5-ounce) can French-style green beans, drained
¼ cup seedless green grapes
¼ teaspoon dried thyme
¼ teaspoon dried marjoram

Slow Cooker Tzimmes

SERVES 8

1. Add the brisket, onion, celery, prunes, and parsley to a 6-quart slow cooker. Mix together the broth, lemon juice, cloves, cinnamon, honey, and vinegar and pour over the meat. Season with salt and pepper to taste. Cover and cook on low 6 hours.
2. Add the sweet potatoes and carrots. Cover and cook on low another 2 hours or until the brisket and vegetables are tender.
3. For a richer sauce, after you remove the meat and vegetables to a serving platter, whisk the butter into the pan juices 1 teaspoon at a time before spooning it over the dish.

1 (3-pound) beef brisket
1 large yellow onion, peeled and chopped
2 stalks celery, chopped
1 (12-ounce) box pitted prunes
1 tablespoon dried or freeze-dried parsley
3 cups beef broth
3 tablespoons fresh lemon juice
¼ teaspoon ground cloves
1 teaspoon ground cinnamon
1 tablespoon honey
2 tablespoons white or white wine vinegar
Salt to taste
Freshly ground black pepper to taste
4 large sweet potatoes, peeled and quartered
1 (1-pound) bag baby carrots
2 tablespoons butter (optional)

VEGETABLE SWAP

To help flavor the broth, add a few chopped carrots during the first 6-hour cooking stage. Omit the remaining carrots called for in the recipe when you add the potatoes. Cover and cook on low 1½ hours. Uncover and add a 12-ounce package frozen cut green beans to the cooker. Cover and cook on low another 30 minutes to steam the vegetables.

Clam Chowder

1. Melt the butter in a 6-quart Dutch oven over medium heat. Add the garlic, celery, and carrots and sauté 2 minutes. Add the onion and sauté until transparent, about 5 minutes.
2. Stir in the pepper, thyme, and flour. Whisk until the butter is absorbed into the flour. Slowly add the broth or water, whisking continuously to blend it with the butter-flour roux. Add the milk, bay leaf, and potatoes.
3. Bring the mixture to a boil; reduce heat, cover, and simmer 10–15 minutes or until the potatoes are tender. Check and stir the chowder frequently to prevent it from burning.
4. Stir in the clams and cream. Bring to temperature, remove the bay leaf, and serve immediately.

½ cup butter
2 cloves garlic, minced
1 stalk celery, finely chopped
2 baby carrots, grated
1 large yellow onion, peeled and diced
½ teaspoon white pepper
⅛ teaspoon dried thyme, crushed
½ cup all-purpose flour
3 cups chicken broth or water
3 cups whole milk
1 bay leaf
4 large russet or red potatoes, peeled or unpeeled, and diced
2 (6.5-ounce) cans chopped or minced clams
2 cups heavy cream

CLAM SALAD

If you have leftover clams don't let them go to waste; use them to make a clam salad. Chop leftover steamed clams and add them to a macaroni salad. For a complete quick and easy lunch, serve it over lettuce and garnish the clam-macaroni salad with chopped fresh parsley or dill.

Fresh Oyster Stew

SERVES 4

1. Shuck the oysters. Start by folding a thick cloth several times to create a square. Use the cloth to steady each oyster firmly on a flat surface as you shuck it; the cloth will also help protect your hand. Insert the tip of an oyster knife between the shell halves and work it around from one side to the other as you pry the shell open. Use a sharp filet or paring knife to cut away the muscles from the flat shell. Bend the shell back, break it off, and discard it. Run the knife underneath the oyster to detach it completely and pour it and the oyster juices into a measuring cup. Discard the bottom shell. Repeat until you have 3 cups.

2. Melt the butter in a heavy 2-quart saucepan over medium heat. Add the onion and sauté until transparent, about 5 minutes. Reduce heat to low and add the milk, cream, salt, and pepper; bring to a light simmer.

3. Add the oysters and juices. Heat only until the oysters are hot; do not overcook. Ladle into bowls and serve immediately. Garnish with parsley.

2 pints fresh oysters
¼ cup butter
1 tablespoon peeled and finely chopped yellow onion or shallot
1 cup whole milk
1 cup heavy cream
Salt to taste
White pepper to taste
Chopped fresh flat-leaf parsley to taste

Moroccan Lamb Stew

SERVES 6

1. Add the lamb to a 6-quart Dutch oven along with the salt, pepper, saffron, ginger, garlic, onion, parsley, and 3 tablespoons of the ghee or oil. Add the water, increasing the amount if necessary to completely cover the meat. Bring to a boil over medium-high heat; lower the heat, cover, and simmer 1½ hours or until the meat is very tender.

2. Add the lemon and cinnamon; cover and simmer 15 minutes. Add the honey and orange blossom water; simmer, stirring frequently, until the sauce is reduced and thickened.

3. If desired, add the remaining tablespoon of ghee or oil to a nonstick skillet and bring to temperature over medium heat. Add the sesame seeds and almonds if using; stir-fry until toasted to a light brown. Garnish each serving with the seed and nut mixture.

2 pounds boneless lamb shoulder, trimmed and cut into 1" cubes
1 teaspoon salt
2 teaspoons freshly ground black pepper
½ teaspoon saffron
1 teaspoon ground ginger
2 cloves garlic, minced
1 large yellow onion, peeled and diced
1 tablespoon dried parsley
4 tablespoons ghee or extra-virgin olive oil, divided
2½ cups water, or more as needed
½ preserved lemon, diced (no pulp)
2 teaspoons ground cinnamon
¼ cup honey
2 tablespoons orange blossom water
1 tablespoon sesame seeds (optional)
¾ cup blanched slivered almonds (optional)

WHERE TO FIND MIDDLE EASTERN INGREDIENTS

Preserved lemon (lemons pickled in a brine of water, lemon juice, and salt) and orange blossom water are available at Middle Eastern markets or from specialty spice shops, such as The Spice House (www.thespicehouse.com). They add the authentic flavors to this dish, which is traditionally served with couscous.

Slow-Cooked Spicy Pork Stew

SERVES 6-8

1. Add the oil to a 4–6-quart slow cooker and bring it to temperature over high. Add the pork; cover and let brown 15 minutes. Stir the pork and brown another 15 minutes. Drain off fat.
2. Add the remaining ingredients except the cilantro or parsley; stir to combine. Reduce heat to low; cover and cook on low 8 hours.
3. Discard the cinnamon stick. Stir in additional chicken broth if the stew is too thick and bring it to temperature. Stir in the cilantro or parsley if desired. Serve warm.

1 tablespoon vegetable oil
2 pounds boneless pork shoulder, trimmed and cut into 1" cubes
1 pound tiny new potatoes, quartered
1 cup peeled and chopped yellow onions
2 poblano peppers, seeded and cut into 1" pieces (optional)
1 jalapeño pepper, seeded and chopped (optional)
4 cloves garlic, minced
1 (2") cinnamon stick
2 cups chicken broth, or more as needed
1 (14.5-ounce) can diced tomatoes
1 tablespoon chili powder
1 teaspoon dried oregano, crushed
¼ teaspoon freshly ground black pepper
¼ cup chopped fresh cilantro or parsley (optional)

HOT PEPPER PRECAUTIONS

Wear gloves or sandwich bags over your hands when you clean and dice hot peppers. It's important to avoid having the peppers come into contact with your skin or your eyes. As an added precaution, wash your hands (don't forget underneath your fingernails) thoroughly with hot soapy water after your remove the gloves or sandwich bags.

CHAPTER 4

Salads and Sides

Beef and Roasted Vegetables with Provençal Vinaigrette

SERVES 4

1. Add the oil, vinegar, parsley, shallot, mustard, salt, and pepper to a glass jar; screw on the lid and shake the jar to combine the dressing. Set aside to allow flavors to meld.
2. In a large microwave-safe bowl, prepare the green beans according to package directions; set aside.
3. Wipe out the bowl and add the potatoes and meat; cover and microwave at 70 percent power for 2 minutes or until heated through. Add the green beans to the bowl and mix with the potatoes and meat.
4. Shake the dressing jar to remix the dressing and then pour it into the bowl; stir to cover the meat and vegetables in the dressing.
5. Add the salad greens, tomatoes, onion, and olives; toss to combine. Serve immediately.

3 tablespoons extra-virgin olive oil

1 tablespoon sherry, red wine, or champagne vinegar

1 tablespoon chopped fresh flat-leaf parsley

2 teaspoons peeled and minced shallot

1 teaspoon Dijon-style mustard

Salt to taste

¼ teaspoon freshly ground black pepper

1 (12-ounce) package frozen green beans

4 small baked or oven-roasted potatoes, quartered

2 cups cubed or shredded leftover steak or roast beef

4 cups mixed baby salad greens

1 cup grape tomatoes

¼ cup peeled and thinly sliced red onion

16 niçoise olives, pitted

Chicken Salad with Toasted Pecans and Green Grapes

SERVES 4

1. Add the sour cream, mayonnaise, vinegar, sugar, onion, and pickles to a large bowl; stir to combine. Fold in the chicken, tomatoes, grapes, and half of the pecans.
2. To serve, put 1 cup salad greens on each of 4 plates. Spoon equal amounts of the chicken salad over the tops of each plate of salad greens, and sprinkle the remaining pecans over the top of the chicken salad.

2/3 cup sour cream
1/3 cup mayonnaise
1/2 teaspoon champagne or white wine vinegar
1 teaspoon granulated sugar
1 small red onion, peeled and diced
8 slices bread and butter pickles, minced
2 cups cubed or shredded cooked chicken
1 cup grape tomatoes
1 cup green seedless grapes
1 cup chopped toasted pecans
4 cups salad mix

TOASTING PECANS

To toast pecans, either dry-fry them 5 minutes in a skillet over medium heat or bake them at 300°F for 10–15 minutes in a single layer on a baking sheet. Either way, be sure to stir them often and only toast them until they just begin to turn brown. Watch the nuts closely, because they go from toasted to burned within seconds, and they'll continue to roast after they've been removed from the heat.

New Orleans–Style Oysters and Shrimp Salad

SERVES 8

1. In a Dutch oven, cook the penne according to package directions; drain, set aside, and keep warm.
2. Wipe out the Dutch oven; add the oil and bring it to temperature over medium heat. Stir in the flour and cook until it begins to turn light brown. Add the yellow onion and sauté 3 minutes or until limp.
3. Whisk in the anchovy paste, milk, and cream. Bring to a simmer and stir in the hot sauce, Worcestershire, and thyme; simmer 10 minutes.
4. Add the oysters and shrimp to the cream sauce. Simmer just long enough to bring the seafood to temperature, then stir in the pasta. If the pasta mixture is too thick, stir in a little extra milk, cream, or liquid drained from the oysters. Add salt and pepper to taste.
5. To serve, spread 1 cup salad mix over the top of each serving plate, ladle pasta mixture over the top, and garnish with green onions.

1 pound dried penne pasta
2 tablespoons peanut or vegetable oil
2 tablespoons all-purpose flour
1 large yellow onion, peeled and diced
1 teaspoon anchovy paste
1 cup whole milk
1 cup heavy cream
Hot sauce to taste
1 teaspoon Worcestershire sauce
Pinch dried thyme
2 pints small oysters, drained
2 pounds medium shrimp, cooked, peeled, and deveined
Salt to taste
Freshly ground black pepper to taste
8 cups salad mix
8 green onions, chopped

Tabouleh

SERVES 4

1. In a large bowl, pour the cold water over the bulgur wheat; let soak 15 minutes. Drain off any excess water and pour the bulgur out onto a clean cotton towel and squeeze dry.
2. Cut off the root end and remove the outer membrane of each green onion. Slice the white part of each green onion into 2 (1") pieces; discard the remaining green parts. Remove the parsley leaves from the stems; discard the stems. Add the green onions, parsley, bell pepper, celery, and mint to a food processor; pulse until finely chopped.
3. Add the oil, lemon juice, allspice, cinnamon, salt, and black pepper to the large bowl. Whisk to mix, and then whisk in the mixture from the food processor. Fold in the bulgur wheat and tomatoes. Serve over salad mix or baby spinach if desired.

1 cup fine bulgur wheat
2 cups cold water
8 green onions
2 large bunches fresh flat-leaf parsley
1 small yellow bell pepper, seeded and quartered
2 stalks celery, cut into quarters
2 tablespoons fresh mint
¼ cup extra-virgin olive oil
¼ cup fresh lemon juice
¼ teaspoon ground allspice
¼ teaspoon ground cinnamon
Salt to taste
¼ teaspoon freshly ground black pepper
4 medium tomatoes, diced
4 cups salad mix or baby spinach (optional)

Indian Spinach Salad

SERVES 8

1. In a large bowl, mix together the yogurt, sour cream, cumin, coriander, black pepper, cayenne, salt, frozen spinach, cucumbers, mint, cilantro, currants or raisins, and nuts. The moisture remaining in the spinach and cucumbers will determine the final texture of the salad; if it's too thick, add additional sour cream to thin it.

2. For each serving, put 1 cup baby spinach on a plate or in a salad bowl and top with a helping of the salad.

1½ cups plain yogurt
½ cup sour cream
1 teaspoon ground cumin, pan-toasted
1 teaspoon ground coriander, pan-toasted
¼ teaspoon freshly ground black pepper
Cayenne pepper to taste
Salt to taste
1 (10-ounce) package frozen spinach, thawed and squeezed dry
2 large cucumbers, peeled and grated
2 tablespoons finely chopped fresh mint
2 tablespoons finely chopped fresh cilantro
½ cup currants or raisins
¼ cup chopped toasted walnuts
½ cup roasted cashews
¼ cup chopped toasted almonds
¼ cup toasted pistachios
¼ cup chopped macadamia nuts
8 cups fresh baby spinach

PAN-TOASTING SPICES

To toast spices on the stovetop, add them to a dry skillet over medium heat and cook until they just begin to release their aromas. Pan-toasting the spices gives them a unique flavor. Be careful not to burn the spices.

Thai Beef Salad

SERVES 4

1. Add the yellow onion, lime juice, fish sauce, mint, sugar, red chili paste, garlic, and beef to a medium bowl; stir to mix. Cover and chill 30 minutes.
2. For each serving, place 1 cup salad mix on a plate or in a salad bowl. Arrange the cucumber slices over the top of the salad mix. Spoon the beef mixture over the cucumber slices. Garnish with cilantro and green onion.

1 small yellow onion, thinly sliced
¼ cup fresh lime juice
¼ cup fish sauce
10 fresh mint leaves, chopped
½ teaspoon granulated sugar
½ teaspoon red chili paste
2 cloves garlic, minced
2 cups cubed cooked beef
4 cups salad mix
2 large cucumbers, thinly sliced
Chopped fresh cilantro to taste
4 green onions, chopped

Macadamia and Avocado Chicken Salad

SERVES 4

1. Add the oil, vinegar, mustard, onions, salt, and black pepper to a large bowl; whisk to combine.
2. Add the chicken, red and yellow bell pepper, nuts, and greens; toss to mix.
3. Spoon the salad onto 4 plates and arrange ¼ of the avocado slices decoratively on the side of each plate.

½ cup macadamia nut oil
2 tablespoons white balsamic vinegar
½ tablespoon whole-grain mustard
2 green onions (white part only), chopped
Salt to taste
Freshly ground black pepper to taste
2 cups shredded cooked chicken
1 medium red bell pepper, seeded and diced
1 medium yellow bell pepper, seeded and diced
4 ounces macadamia nuts, chopped
4 cups mesclun greens
2 medium avocados, peeled, pitted, and sliced

Swedish Herring Salad

SERVES 4

1. Add the diced potatoes and water to a large microwave-safe bowl; cover and microwave on high 5 minutes or until the potatoes are tender. Drain in a colander and then return to the bowl.
2. Drain the beets, reserving 6 tablespoons of the liquid; finely dice the beets and add to the bowl. Peel the hard-boiled eggs and reserve the yolks for another use; dice the whites and add them to the bowl.
3. Drain and finely chop the herring; add to the bowl along with the apple, beef, onion, dill pickle, reserved beet liquid, vinegar, 1 tablespoon sugar, salt, and black pepper. Mix well; taste for seasoning and add the remaining sugar if desired.
4. Whip the heavy cream until soft peaks form; fold it into the salad.
5. Garnish with chopped green onions and serve as is or over salad mix if desired.

½ pound new potatoes, unpeeled, diced small
½ cup water
1 (1-pound) can pickled beets
2 large hard-boiled eggs
2 (6-ounce) jars wine-flavored pickled herring
1 medium Granny Smith apple, cored and diced small
½ cup shredded cooked roast beef
2 tablespoons yellow onion, peeled and finely diced
⅓ cup finely chopped dill pickle
2 tablespoons white or white wine vinegar
1–2 tablespoons granulated sugar
Salt to taste
Freshly ground black pepper to taste
½ cup heavy cream
4 cups salad mix (optional)
Chopped green onion to taste

Chicken and Cellophane Noodle Salad

SERVES 4

1. Add the noodles and chicken broth to a saucepan; soak the noodles 1 hour. Place the saucepan over medium heat and bring to a simmer; simmer 10 minutes or until the noodles are tender. Drain off the broth. Cover and cool in the refrigerator.

2. Add the peanut butter, hot water, soy sauce, and red chili paste or cayenne to a small bowl; whisk to mix, adding more water if necessary to bring the mixture to the consistency of heavy cream. Pour the mixture over the noodles; toss to mix.

3. Peel, seed, and cut the cucumbers into julienne strips. In a small bowl, mix together the cucumbers, vinegar, sugar, and sesame oil.

4. To assemble each salad, arrange 1 cup salad mix on a plate or in a salad bowl. Top with ¼ of the cellophane noodles, ¼ of the chicken, ¼ of the cucumber, and 1 tablespoon peanuts.

1 (8-ounce) package cellophane noodles
2 cups chicken broth
¼ cup peanut butter
2 tablespoons hot water
5 tablespoons soy sauce
Red chili paste or cayenne pepper to taste
2 large cucumbers
1 tablespoon rice wine vinegar
½ teaspoon granulated sugar
2 teaspoons sesame oil
4 cups salad mix
2 cups shredded cooked chicken
¼ cup chopped dry-roasted peanuts

A NOODLE BY ANY OTHER NAME

Cellophane noodles—sometimes referred to as bean threads, glass noodles, and sai fun—are commonly made from bean starch. These delicate noodles easily absorb the flavors they are cooked with. You can find them in the Asian foods aisle in most supermarkets.

Chicken Waldorf Salad

SERVES 4

1. Add the mayonnaise, sour cream, lime juice, sugar, and ginger to a large bowl; stir to combine, then fold in the apples, celery, walnuts, and chicken. Add salt and pepper to taste.
2. To serve, spoon ¼ of the chicken salad over 1 cup salad mix.

¼ cup mayonnaise
½ cup sour cream
½ tablespoon fresh lime juice
1 teaspoon granulated sugar
¼ teaspoon grated fresh ginger
1 large Granny Smith apple, cored and diced
1 large Red Delicious apple, cored and diced
1 large Yellow Delicious apple, cored and diced
2 stalks celery, diced
½ cup chopped toasted walnuts
2 cups shredded cooked chicken
Salt to taste
Freshly ground black pepper to taste
4 cups salad mix

Bacon–Spinach Salad

SERVES 4

1. Add the oil, onion, sugar, vinegar, ketchup, and Worcestershire to a blender or food processor; pulse to mix.
2. To assemble each salad, arrange 2 cups spinach on a plate and top with the mushrooms, eggs, bacon, and bean sprouts (if using). Drizzle a generous amount of dressing over the salad and top with grated cheese. Refrigerate any leftover dressing.

1 cup vegetable oil
1 small yellow or red onion, peeled and diced
¾ cup granulated sugar
¼ cup apple cider vinegar
⅓ cup ketchup
1 teaspoon Worcestershire sauce
8 cups baby spinach, stems removed
8 ounces button mushrooms, sliced
4 large hard-boiled eggs, peeled and chopped
8 slices bacon, cooked crisp and crumbled
Fresh bean sprouts (optional)
4 ounces Cheddar cheese, grated

Tuna–Macaroni Salad

SERVES 4

1. Add the cooked macaroni to a large bowl. Add the cheese, tuna, pickles, onion, salad dressing or mayonnaise, sugar, salt, and pepper. Stir to combine. Cover and refrigerate overnight.
2. Serve the salad on top of lettuce leaves or salad mix if desired.

7 ounces cooked elbow macaroni
4 ounces Cheddar cheese, cut into cubes
1 (7-ounce) can tuna, drained
¾ cup chopped candied sweet pickles
1 small red onion, peeled and diced
1 cup salad dressing or mayonnaise
1 tablespoon granulated sugar, or to taste
Salt to taste
Freshly ground black pepper to taste
Iceberg lettuce or salad mix (optional)

Rotisserie Chicken Salad

SERVES 4

1. Cut the legs, thighs, and wings from the chicken. Remove and discard the skin from the rest of the chicken; remove the remaining meat from the chicken and shred it.
2. Place 2 cups salad mix on each of 4 plates. Divide the shredded chicken between the plates, placing it atop the salad mix. Place a leg or thigh on each plate.
3. Add the vinegar, mustard, garlic, salt, pepper, and oil to a jar; cover and shake vigorously to emulsify. Pour the dressing evenly over the chicken-topped salad mix on each plate. Top each salad with grated cheese if desired.

1 (3-pound) Italian-seasoned rotisserie chicken
8 cups salad mix
2 tablespoons red wine vinegar
1 tablespoon Dijon mustard
1 clove garlic, minced
¼ teaspoon sea salt
¼ teaspoon freshly ground black pepper
¼ cup extra-virgin olive oil
Freshly grated Parmigiano-Reggiano cheese to taste (optional)

AS MOIST AND JUICY AS A ROTISSERIE CHICKEN

You can prepare a beer-can-style chicken instead of using a rotisserie. Place a Chicken Rocket (www.chickenrocket.com) or Beer Can Chicken Roaster (www.mrbarbq.com) in a seasoned cast-iron skillet or roasting pan large enough to hold the chicken and vegetables. Fill the reservoir to the halfway mark with seasoned chicken broth or beer, season the chicken according to the recipe, place it on the roasting stand, and bake at 400°F for 1½ hours.

Shrimp Salad with Louis Dressing

SERVES 4

1. To make the Louis Dressing, add the mayonnaise, spinach, watercress, onion, garlic, lemon juice, and sugar to a blender or food processor; pulse until smooth. Cover and chill until ready to assemble the salad.
2. For each salad serving, put 1 cup salad mix on a serving plate and top with 1 sliced tomato, 1 sliced hard-boiled egg, and ¼ of the shrimp. Season with salt and pepper to taste, and top with the Louis Dressing.

1 cup mayonnaise
½ cup fresh spinach leaves
5 sprigs watercress
½ small yellow onion, peeled
1 clove garlic, minced
1 tablespoon fresh lemon juice
1½ teaspoons granulated sugar
4 cups lettuce or salad mix
4 small tomatoes, sliced
4 large hard-boiled eggs, peeled and sliced
1 pound cooked shrimp, peeled, deveined, and cooled
Salt to taste
Freshly ground black pepper to taste

Quinoa and Spinach Salad

SERVES 2

1. Cover the quinoa with water; rub the grains between the palms of your hands for several seconds, drain, and repeat the process once.
2. Bring the water to a boil in a saucepan; add the quinoa, salt, and 2 tablespoons oil. Lower heat, cover, and simmer 20 minutes or until all the water is absorbed. Remove the pan from the heat and allow the cooked quinoa to cool, and then fluff with a fork. Stir in the artichoke hearts, olives, spinach, tomatoes, and parsley.
3. To make the citrus vinaigrette, whisk together the lemon zest, balsamic vinegar, orange juice, remaining oil, oregano, mint, basil, and pepper.
4. Divide the spinach between 2 plates and top each with the quinoa salad. Dress with the citrus vinaigrette and serve with the pine nuts and feta cheese sprinkled over the top.

2 cups quinoa
4½ cups water
1 teaspoon sea salt
4 tablespoons extra-virgin olive oil, divided
½ cup sliced marinated artichoke hearts
¼ cup sliced, pitted kalamata olives
2 tablespoons finely chopped fresh spinach
1 cup halved cherry tomatoes
2 tablespoons finely chopped fresh flat-leaf parsley
1 tablespoon freshly grated lemon zest
¼ cup balsamic vinegar, or more to taste
¼ cup orange juice
1 teaspoon dried oregano
1 teaspoon dried mint
1 teaspoon dried fresh basil
Freshly ground black pepper to taste
2 cups fresh baby spinach
2 tablespoons toasted pine nuts
½ cup crumbled feta cheese

Tuna and Fresh Tomato Pizza

SERVES 1

1. Preheat oven to 450°F.
2. Coat both sides of the tortilla with the oil. Place on a baking sheet.
3. Add the tomato to a small bowl and mix it with the sugar. Spread the tomato and juices over the tortilla. Sprinkle the garlic, onion, oregano, basil, parsley, salt, and pepper over the tomato. Add as much of the tuna as you wish, and top with the cheeses.
4. Bake 5 minutes or until the cheese is melted and bubbly. Drizzle more extra-virgin olive oil over the top of the baked pizza if desired.

1 (8") flour tortilla
Extra-virgin olive oil to taste
1 small vine-ripened tomato, peeled and chopped
Pinch granulated sugar
Pinch dried minced garlic or garlic powder
Pinch dried minced onion or onion powder
Pinch dried oregano
Pinch dried basil
Pinch dried parsley
Salt to taste
Freshly ground black pepper to taste
1 (12-ounce) can reduced-sodium tuna, drained
Shredded mozzarella cheese to taste
Freshly grated Parmigiano-Reggiano cheese to taste

Cuban Black Beans

SERVES 4-6

1. Rinse the beans and put them in a 6-quart Dutch oven with the 4 cups water. Bring to a boil over medium-high heat; cover and boil 2 minutes. Turn off the heat and let sit 1 hour.
2. Add the garlic, green pepper, onion, salt pork or bacon, ham hocks, paprika, cumin, bay leaves, broth, and chili powder. Add enough additional water so that the beans are completely covered. Cover and simmer 2 hours over low heat or until the beans are tender.
3. Remove the ham hocks and take the meat off of the bones; return the meat to the pan. Remove and discard the bay leaves. Add the vinegar, salt, and pepper, and stir to mix.

1 pound dried black beans
4 cups water, or more as needed
3 cloves garlic, minced
1 medium green bell pepper, seeded and chopped
1 large yellow onion, peeled and chopped
½ pound salt pork or bacon, chopped
1 pound smoked ham hocks
2 teaspoons paprika
1 tablespoon ground cumin
2 bay leaves
4 cups chicken broth
¼ teaspoon chili powder
1 tablespoon red wine vinegar
Salt to taste
Freshly ground black pepper to taste

USING LEFTOVERS

It's easy to turn Cuban Black Beans into a satisfying soup. Once the beans are tender, simply add more chicken broth and bring to temperature. After you've added the vinegar, salt, and pepper, taste for seasoning and adjust by adding more vinegar and other seasonings if needed.

Southwest Pinto Beans with Pork and Corn

SERVES 4-6

1. Add the bacon to a deep nonstick skillet or large saucepan; fry over medium heat until it begins to brown. Add the onion and sauté until transparent, about 5–7 minutes. Add the garlic and chopped pepper (if using), and sauté 1 minute.
2. Stir in the beans, corn, and pork. Bring to a simmer and cook 5–10 minutes until heated through. Add salt and pepper to taste.

4 slices bacon, diced
1 large yellow onion, peeled and diced
3 cloves garlic, minced
Chopped jalapeño or other hot pepper to taste (optional)
1 (15-ounce) can pinto beans, rinsed and drained
1 (12-ounce) bag frozen whole-kernel corn, thawed
1 (28-ounce) can heat-and-serve pork in pork broth
Salt to taste
Freshly ground black pepper to taste

CHAPTER 5

Poultry Entrées

Chicken, Tortellini, and Broccoli Casserole

SERVES 8

1. Preheat oven to 325°F.
2. In an ovenproof Dutch oven, cook the tortellini according to package directions; drain and keep warm.
3. Wipe out the Dutch oven. Add the oil and bring it to temperature over medium-high heat. Add the broccoli, onion, and bell pepper and stir-fry about 3 minutes or until crisp-tender. Remove the broccoli from the skillet; set it aside with the cooked tortellini and keep warm. Reduce heat to low and whisk the flour into the oil and remaining vegetables in the pan, stirring constantly, until smooth.
4. Stir in the broth, milk, and parsley. Bring to a boil over medium heat, stirring constantly; remove from heat.
5. Stir in the chicken, Monterey jack, tortellini, and broccoli. Bake uncovered 30 minutes or until bubbly. Sprinkle the Colby over the top of the casserole; return to the oven and bake 10 minutes or until the cheese topping is melted.

1 (9-ounce) package cheese tortellini
3 tablespoons extra-virgin olive oil
2 cups broccoli florets
1 medium yellow onion, peeled and diced
1 medium red bell pepper, seeded and diced
3 tablespoons all-purpose flour
¾ cup chicken broth
¾ cup whole milk
1 teaspoon dried parsley
4 cups diced cooked chicken
6 ounces Monterey jack cheese, grated
4 ounces Colby cheese, grated

GRATED CHEESE

Each ounce of soft cheese like Cheddar or Colby equals ¼ cup of grated cheese. Keep this in mind when you go to the grocery store and pick up the bags of preshredded cheese. They'll tell you the weight but not the measurement in cups, so it's up to you to remember that part.

Stuffed Chicken Breast Florentine with Button Mushrooms

SERVES 8

1. Preheat oven to 350°F.
2. Place each chicken breast between 2 pieces of plastic wrap; pound until about ½" thick. Brush the bottom of a 9" × 13" nonstick baking pan with 1 tablespoon oil. Arrange half of the chicken breasts over the bottom of the pan.
3. Add the mushrooms, garlic, and shallots to a large microwave-safe bowl. Toss with the remaining 2 tablespoons oil. Cover and microwave on high 1 minute; stir. Cover and microwave 1 more minute. Let cool and then stir in the spinach. Add the eggs, 2 cups bread crumbs, cheese, parsley, and broth; stir to combine.
4. Arrange half of the deli ham over the top of the chicken breasts in the pan. Spread the spinach mixture over the top of the ham, then top with the remaining ham. Place the remaining chicken breasts over the top of the ham. Season with salt and pepper. Tightly cover the pan with foil. Bake 45 minutes.
5. Melt the butter and mix it with the remaining bread crumbs. Remove the foil from the pan and sprinkle the buttered bread crumbs over the top of the chicken. Return to the oven and bake uncovered 15 minutes or until the bread crumbs are golden brown and the chicken breasts are cooked through. Remove from oven and let sit 10 minutes, then cut into 8 equal pieces and serve.

8 (4-ounce) boneless, skinless chicken breasts
3 tablespoons extra-virgin olive oil, divided
8 ounces button mushrooms, sliced
2 cloves garlic, minced
3 tablespoons peeled and chopped shallots
2 (10-ounce) packages frozen spinach, thawed and squeezed dry
4 large eggs, beaten
3 cups bread crumbs, divided
4 ounces Swiss or mozzarella cheese, shredded
2 tablespoons dried parsley
1 cup chicken broth
¼ pound deli ham, thinly sliced
Salt to taste
Freshly ground black pepper to taste
¼ cup butter

Chicken Paprikash Medley

SERVES 8

1. In a large Dutch oven bring the butter and oil to temperature over medium-high heat. Add the onion and sauté 3 minutes. Add the chicken to the Dutch oven and stir-fry 5 minutes. Stir in the garlic, salt, pepper, 3 tablespoons paprika, and 3½ cups broth; cover the pan and bring to a boil.

2. While the chicken broth comes to a boil, mix the remaining ½ cup chicken broth with the flour. Strain out any lumps, and then whisk the broth mixture into the boiling broth. Boil 3 minutes. Stir in the broccoli stir-fry mix; lower heat, cover, and simmer 5 minutes.

3. Remove the pan from the burner and stir in the sour cream. Pour the chicken and vegetable mixture over the noodles or spaetzle. Sprinkle the remaining tablespoon of paprika over the top. Serve immediately.

1 tablespoon butter
1 tablespoon extra-virgin olive oil
1 large yellow onion, peeled and diced
1½ pounds boneless, skinless chicken breasts, cut into bite-sized pieces
4 cloves garlic, minced
Salt to taste
Freshly ground black pepper to taste
4 tablespoons Hungarian paprika, divided
4 cups chicken broth, divided
2 tablespoons all-purpose flour
1 (16-ounce) bag frozen broccoli stir-fry mix, thawed
16 ounces sour cream
4 cups cooked egg noodles or spaetzle

THICKENING OR THINNING

The temperature at which you simmer the paprikash will affect how thick or thin the sauce gets. The sour cream added at the end of the cooking time will also thicken the sauce. If the sauce is too thin, add more sour cream. If it's too thick, slowly whisk in some additional chicken broth, milk, or water.

Italian Stuffed Chicken

SERVES 4

1. Preheat oven to 375°F.
2. Add the potatoes to a medium microwave-safe bowl; cover and microwave on high 5 minutes. Add the olives, parsley, garlic, anchovies, capers, olive oil, salt, and pepper to the potatoes and stir to combine.
3. Rinse the chicken inside and out. Dry the chicken with paper towels, then stuff the chicken with the hot potato mixture. Place the chicken on a rack in a roasting pan.
4. Brush the outside of the chicken with the melted butter. Season with salt and pepper to taste. Sprinkle the rosemary over the chicken.
5. Bake 80–90 minutes. Remove from the oven and let rest 10 minutes. Cut into quarters and serve with the potato stuffing.

4 medium russet potatoes, diced
10 pimiento-stuffed green olives, chopped
1 tablespoon dried parsley
2 cloves garlic, minced
3 canned flat anchovies, mashed (optional)
1 tablespoon capers, rinsed and chopped
3 tablespoons olive oil
Salt to taste
Freshly ground black pepper to taste
1 (3-pound) chicken
1 tablespoon butter, melted
Dried rosemary to taste

IMPROVISED ROASTING RACK

If your roasting pan doesn't have a removable rack, arrange stalks of celery, curved-side down, over the bottom of the pan and place the meat on top of the celery. This adds enough height to allow some of the fat to drain away from the meat.

Chicken Divan

SERVES 6

1. Preheat oven to 350°F.
2. Melt the butter over medium heat in a 2-quart or larger ovenproof skillet or Dutch oven. Add the flour and cook, stirring constantly, 1 minute.
3. Gradually whisk in the broth and milk; cook 3 minutes or until it begins to thicken. Stir in salt, pepper, nutmeg, 1/4 cup of the cheese, and sherry; cook until the cheese melts. Remove from the heat and stir in the chicken, broccoli, half of the almonds, and the cream. Sprinkle the remaining almonds, cheese, and bread cubes over the top.
4. Bake uncovered 35 minutes or until bubbly and golden brown.

¼ cup butter
¼ cup all-purpose flour
1 cup chicken broth
1 cup whole milk
Salt to taste
Freshly ground black pepper to taste
⅛ teaspoon ground nutmeg
½ cup freshly grated Parmigiano-Reggiano cheese, divided
3 tablespoons dry sherry
3 cups cubed cooked chicken
1 (16-ounce) bag broccoli florets, thawed
1 cup slivered almonds, divided
½ cup heavy cream
1 cup bread cubes

SHAKE UP YOUR CHICKEN DIVAN

For a lighter sauce, whip the cream until it reaches soft peaks and then fold it into the other Chicken Divan ingredients before you top the casserole with the remaining almonds and cheese. If you don't have heavy cream on hand, you can substitute sour cream or melt 4 ounces of cream cheese into the sauce before you add the chicken.

Chicken Braised with Sweet Peppers

SERVES 4

1. Add the oil to a deep 3½-quart nonstick skillet and bring to temperature over medium heat. Add the chicken; fry about 5 minutes, turning the chicken so it browns evenly. Drain and discard any excess fat.
2. Add the broth, wine, garlic, rosemary, salt, and black pepper to the skillet. Bring to a boil; reduce heat, cover, and simmer 20 minutes.
3. Add the tomatoes, bell peppers, and mushrooms to the skillet. Cover and simmer another 15 minutes or until the chicken is tender and no longer pink. Transfer the chicken to a serving dish; cover with foil and keep warm.
4. Add the cornstarch and water to a small bowl; stir to combine. Mix in 1 or 2 tablespoons of the hot broth to thin the cornstarch mixture and then gently stir the mixture into the broth and vegetables. Continue to cook 3 minutes or until the sauce is thickened and has lost its raw cornstarch flavor.
5. Spoon the vegetables and sauce around chicken. Serve with noodles or rice.

1 tablespoon extra-virgin olive or vegetable oil
8 small bone-in chicken thighs, skin removed
⅔ cup chicken broth
¼ cup dry white wine
2 cloves garlic, minced
¼ teaspoon dried rosemary, crushed
Salt to taste
¼ teaspoon freshly ground black pepper
1 (15-ounce) can diced tomatoes
1 small yellow bell pepper, cut into ½" strips
1 small green bell pepper, cut into ½" strips
1 small red bell pepper, cut into ½" strips
8 ounces button mushrooms, sliced
2 tablespoons cornstarch
2 tablespoons cold water
2 cups hot cooked noodles or rice

Ginger Chicken and Vegetable Stir-Fry

SERVES 4

1. In a small bowl, make the sauce by stirring together the water, soy sauce, hoisin, cornstarch, ginger, and sesame oil. Set aside.
2. Add the peanut oil to a wok or large skillet and bring to temperature over medium-high heat. Add the chicken pieces and stir-fry 5 minutes or until the chicken is cooked through. Push the chicken to the edges of the pan; add the stir-fry mix and pepper strips and stir-fry 3 minutes or until the vegetables are crisp-tender.
3. Push the chicken and vegetables away from the center of pan. Pour the sauce mixture into the center of pan; cook and stir until thickened and bubbly. Stir the sauce into the chicken and vegetables. Serve over chow mein noodles or rice.

½ cup water
2 tablespoons soy sauce
2 tablespoons hoisin sauce
2 teaspoons cornstarch
1 teaspoon grated fresh ginger
1 teaspoon toasted sesame oil
2 tablespoons peanut oil
12 ounces skinless, boneless chicken, cut into bite-sized pieces
1 (16-ounce) bag frozen broccoli stir-fry mix, thawed
1 medium yellow bell pepper, seeded and cut into strips
2 cups chow mein noodles or hot cooked rice

Slow-Cooked Chicken with Creamy Lemon Sauce

SERVES 4

1. Place the green beans and onion in a 3-quart or larger slow cooker. Arrange the chicken and potatoes over the vegetables. Sprinkle with the garlic and pepper. Pour the broth over the top. Cover and cook on low 5 hours or until the chicken is cooked through and moist.
2. Transfer the chicken and vegetables to 4 serving plates or a serving platter; cover to keep warm.
3. To make the sauce, add the cream cheese and grated lemon peel to the broth in the slow cooker. Stir until the cheese melts into the sauce. Pour the sauce over the chicken and vegetables. Garnish with lemon peel strips if desired.

1 (16-ounce) bag frozen cut green beans, thawed
1 small yellow onion, peeled and cut into thin wedges
4 (4-ounce) boneless, skinless chicken breast halves
4 medium russet potatoes, peeled and quartered
2 cloves garlic, minced
¼ teaspoon freshly ground black pepper
1 cup chicken broth
4 ounces cream cheese, cut into cubes
1 teaspoon freshly grated lemon peel
Lemon peel strips (optional)

THE WORLD'S EASIEST VEGETABLE DISH

When they're prepared correctly, you'd swear that freeze-dried green beans taste as good as fresh. About 5–10 minutes before you plan to serve them, pour boiling water over the freeze-dried green beans so that they're completely submerged. When you're ready to serve them, drain and toss the green beans with a little fresh lemon juice, extra-virgin olive oil, salt, and freshly ground black pepper.

Greek Meat and Vegetable Pie

SERVES 8

1. Preheat oven to 350°F.
2. Add the onions and oil to a large microwave-safe bowl. Cover and microwave on high 1 minute. Stir, cover, and then microwave 2 minutes or until transparent. Add the spinach to the bowl and toss with the onions. Microwave the broccoli according to the package directions; drain and add to the bowl. Add the cheese, eggs, chicken or turkey, chives, dill, parsley, and pepper to the bowl and mix well. Set aside to cool.
3. Brush the bottom of a 9" × 13" nonstick baking pan with some of the butter. Layer half of the phyllo sheets on the bottom, 1 sheet at a time, brushing each sheet with butter before adding the next sheet. Evenly spread the meat and vegetable filling over the buttered phyllo sheets. Top the filling with the remaining sheets, brushing each sheet with butter before you add the next sheet. Cut into 8 equal pieces.
4. Bake uncovered 1 hour or until golden brown.

1 medium yellow onion, peeled and diced
2 green onions, diced
2 tablespoons extra-virgin olive oil
1 (8-ounce) bag baby spinach, torn
1 (12-ounce) bag frozen steam-in-the-
   bag broccoli florets
8 ounces crumbled feta cheese
2 large eggs
2 cups diced cooked chicken or turkey
2 tablespoons minced fresh chives
2 tablespoons minced fresh dill
½ cup minced fresh flat-leaf parsley
Freshly ground black pepper to taste
½ cup butter, melted
1 (16-ounce) package phyllo dough

Slow-Cooked Chicken Cacciatore

SERVES 6

1. Add the mushrooms, celery, carrot, onions, bell pepper, and garlic to a 5- or 6-quart slow cooker. Place chicken on top of vegetables.
2. Mix the broth, wine, tapioca, sugar, oregano, bay leaves, salt, and pepper in a small bowl; pour over chicken. Cover and cook on low 6–7 hours or until the chicken is cooked through.
3. Remove and discard bay leaves. Remove the chicken to a serving platter; cover and keep warm. Turn the slow cooker to the high setting. Stir in the undrained tomatoes and the tomato paste. Cover and cook 15 minutes. Pour the resulting sauce over the chicken. Serve with cooked pasta or rice.

8 ounces button or cremini mushrooms, sliced
3 stalks celery, sliced
3 large carrots, peeled and diced
2 medium yellow onions, peeled and sliced
1 large red bell pepper, cut into strips
4 cloves garlic, minced
12 bone-in, skinless chicken thighs or drumsticks
1/2 cup chicken broth
1/4 cup dry white wine
2 tablespoons quick-cooking tapioca
1 teaspoon granulated sugar
1 teaspoon dried oregano, crushed
2 bay leaves
1/2 teaspoon salt
1/4 teaspoon freshly ground black pepper
1 (14.5-ounce) can diced tomatoes
1/3 cup tomato paste
Hot cooked pasta or rice

BAKED LONG-GRAIN WHITE RICE

Chicken Cacciatore is delicious served over baked rice. In an ovenproof 8-cup saucepan or skillet, sauté 1 medium diced onion in 2 tablespoons butter. Add 1 cup rinsed long-grain white rice and 2 cups chicken broth. Bring to a boil, cover, and then bake at 325°F for 20 minutes. Makes about 3 1/2 cups cooked rice.

Chicken in Button Mushroom Gravy

SERVES 6

1. Preheat oven to 425°F.
2. Coat the chicken in the flour and arrange skin-side down in the melted butter in a 9" × 13" nonstick baking pan. Add the potatoes to the pan. Bake 30 minutes. Use tongs to turn the chicken, reduce the oven temperature to 325°F, and bake an additional 30 minutes.
3. Add the evaporated milk, soup, cheese, salt, and pepper to a bowl; stir to mix. Remove the potatoes from the baking pan, wrap in foil, and return to the oven. Drain any excess fat from the chicken and discard.
4. Arrange the peas and onions over the chicken, then top with the mushrooms. Evenly pour the evaporated milk mixture over the mushrooms. Sprinkle with paprika. Cover the baking pan with foil, return to the oven, and bake 20 minutes.

12 small bone-in, skin-on chicken thighs
¼ cup all-purpose flour
¼ cup butter, melted
6 medium russet potatoes, pierced with a fork
1 cup evaporated milk
1 (10¾-ounce) can condensed cream of mushroom soup
4 ounces American cheese, grated
Salt to taste
Freshly ground black pepper to taste
1 (16-ounce) bag frozen baby peas and pearl onions, thawed
4 ounces button mushrooms, sliced
Paprika to taste

SERVING SUGGESTION
If you want to avoid adding extra butter to the baked potatoes in this dish, put each potato on a serving plate, cut it in half lengthwise, and lightly mash the pulp. Spoon the vegetable-gravy mixture over the potato and place a chicken thigh over the top of each half.

Curried Chicken with Avocado

SERVES 6

1. Melt the butter and bring it to temperature in a nonstick skillet over medium heat. Add the chicken, onion, salt, and pepper and sauté until the chicken is cooked through, about 8–10 minutes.
2. Add the apple, garlic, and curry powder and sauté 2 minutes. Stir in the flour; whisk the cream and then the broth into the chicken mixture. Bring to a boil and boil 2 minutes.
3. To serve, place an avocado half on top of ½ cup cooked rice and spoon the hot chicken curry over the avocado.

¼ cup butter
1 pound boneless, skinless chicken breasts, cut into bite-sized pieces
1 small yellow onion, peeled and diced
Salt to taste
Freshly ground black pepper to taste
1 Golden Delicious apple, peeled, cored, and thinly sliced
1 clove garlic, minced
1 tablespoon curry powder
¼ cup all-purpose flour
1 cup heavy or light cream
1 cup chicken broth
3 large avocados, peeled, pitted, and halved
3 cups cooked rice

OPTIONAL CONDIMENTS

This dish is good served with chopped hard-boiled egg, chopped peanuts, chutney, coconut, crumbled crisp bacon, preserved ginger, raisins, and sweet pickles as condiments. Try something new or just use whatever you have in your pantry.

Herb-Roasted Chicken with Oven-Roasted Root Vegetables

SERVES 4

1. Heat oven to 450°F. Place an ovenproof 6- or 8-quart Dutch into oven to heat.
2. Rinse the inside and outside of the chicken and pat it dry. Halve 1 lemon; stuff the chicken with the lemon halves and smashed garlic cloves.
3. To truss the chicken, cut kitchen twine to five times the length of the chicken. Place the middle section of the string under the tail and wrap the tail. Next, wrap the ends of the string around the ends of each drumstick. Pull the string to draw the legs together, crossing the strings over one another to secure the legs in this position. Turn the chicken over. Tie the string across the wings to hold them in place. Cut off any excess string.
4. Juice the remaining lemon and add with oil, basil, thyme, parsley, minced garlic, salt, and pepper to a large bowl and mix well. Rub 2 tablespoons over outside of the chicken.
5. Transfer chicken to the Dutch oven. Roast 45 minutes.
6. Add the turnips, carrots, beets, and potatoes to the large bowl and toss to coat in the herb-oil mixture. Carefully pour vegetables into the Dutch oven and roast another 30 minutes or until the juices from the chicken thigh run clear and the internal temperature of the breast and thigh reach 160°F.
7. To serve, drain and discard the excess fat from the potatoes and vegetables. Arrange the potatoes and vegetables on a serving platter. Remove and discard the twine and herbs and lemon and place the chicken on the platter. Cover with foil and let rest 10 minutes before carving.

1 (3-pound) chicken
2 medium lemons
2 cloves garlic, smashed
2 tablespoons extra-virgin olive oil
1 teaspoon dried basil
1 teaspoon dried thyme
1 teaspoon dried parsley
2 cloves garlic, minced
Salt to taste
Freshly ground black pepper to taste
1/4 pound baby turnips, peeled and stem ends trimmed
1/4 pound baby red carrots, peeled and stem ends trimmed
1/4 pound orange carrots, peeled and stem ends trimmed
1/4 pound baby golden beets, peeled and stem ends trimmed
1/4 pound baby beets, peeled and stem ends trimmed
1/4 pound fingerling potatoes, halved

Fusion Stir-Fry

SERVES 4

1. Remove and discard the skin from the chicken; remove the meat from the bones and shred it. In a small bowl, make the sauce by stirring together the water, soy sauce, hoisin, cornstarch, ginger, steak sauce, honey (if using), and sesame oil. Set aside.
2. Heat the rice pouch in the microwave according to package directions.
3. Add the peanut oil to a wok or large skillet and bring to temperature over medium-high heat. Add the stir-fry mix and red pepper and stir-fry 3 minutes or until the vegetables are crisp-tender. Stir in the shredded chicken; stir-fry 2 minutes or until the chicken is heated through.
4. Push the chicken and vegetables away from the center of pan. Pour the sauce mixture into the center of pan; cook and stir until thickened and bubbly. Stir the sauce into the chicken and vegetables. Add the cooked rice and toss to combine.

1 (3-pound) lemon-pepper rotisserie chicken
½ cup water
2 tablespoons soy sauce
2 tablespoons hoisin sauce
2 teaspoons cornstarch
1 teaspoon grated fresh ginger
2 teaspoons steak sauce
1 teaspoon honey (optional)
1 teaspoon toasted sesame oil
1 (8.8-ounce) microwaveable pouch brown rice
1 tablespoon peanut oil
1 (16-pound) bag frozen broccoli stir-fry mix, thawed
1 medium red bell pepper, seeded and cut into strips

Open-Face Chicken and Sautéed Pepper Sandwiches

SERVES 8

1. Remove and discard the skin from the chicken; remove the meat from the bones and shred it.
2. Bring the oil to temperature in a large nonstick skillet. Add the peppers; sauté 3 minutes. Add the onion; sauté 5 minutes or until the onion is transparent. Stir in the garlic, oregano, rosemary, and parsley. Add the wine or broth and vinegar; simmer 5 minutes. Stir in the shredded chicken and simmer 5 more minutes or until the chicken is heated through, the peppers are tender, and most of the wine is evaporated.
3. Add salt and pepper to taste. To serve, evenly spoon the mixture over the top of the toast slices.

1 (3-pound) rotisserie chicken
3 tablespoons extra-virgin olive oil
2 large red bell peppers, seeded and cut into thin strips
2 large orange or yellow bell peppers, seeded and cut into thin strips
2 large green bell peppers, seeded and cut into thin strips
1 large yellow onion, peeled and thinly sliced
3 cloves garlic, minced
1 teaspoon dried oregano, crushed
1 teaspoon chopped dried rosemary
1 tablespoon dried parsley
½ cup dry red wine or ⅓ cup chicken broth and 2 tablespoons balsamic vinegar
Salt to taste
Freshly ground black pepper to taste
8 slices bread, toasted

SEASONING SUGGESTIONS

The herbs used in this recipe go well with an Italian-seasoned rotisserie chicken; however, you may need to adjust the amounts according to how highly seasoned the chicken is. If you're using a lemon-pepper rotisserie chicken, you may wish to omit the herbs suggested in the recipe and replace them with some Mrs. Dash Lemon Pepper Seasoning Blend to taste.

Chicken and Spinach Enchiladas

SERVES 6-12

1. Preheat oven to 350°F. Treat a 9" × 13" nonstick baking pan with nonstick spray.
2. Remove and discard the skin from the chicken; remove the meat from the bones and shred it.
3. For the filling, mix together the shredded chicken, spinach, green onions, salsa, and half of the cheese in a bowl.
4. Soften the flour or corn tortillas by placing them on a microwave-safe plate; cover with a damp paper towel and microwave on high 1 minute. Spoon the filling down the centers of the tortillas, roll them, and place seam-side down in the prepared baking pan.
5. To make the sauce, add the sour cream, flour, salt, pepper, cumin, milk, and chilies to a small bowl; stir to mix. Spoon the sauce over the tops of the rolled tortillas in the baking pan. Cover and bake 20 minutes.
6. Uncover and bake an additional 20 minutes or until heated through. Sprinkle with the remaining cheese; bake another 5 minutes, remove from the oven, and let stand 5 minutes before serving. Garnish with tomato and cilantro if desired.

Nonstick cooking spray
1 (3-pound) rotisserie chicken
1 (10-ounce) package frozen chopped spinach, thawed and well drained
6 green onions, thinly sliced
1 cup tomato salsa
4 ounces Cheddar or Monterey jack cheese, shredded
12 (7") flour or corn tortillas
1¼ cups sour cream
2 tablespoons all-purpose flour
Salt to taste
Freshly ground black pepper to taste
½ teaspoon ground cumin
½ cup whole milk
1 (4-ounce) can diced green chilies, drained
Fresh tomato, diced (optional)
Fresh cilantro, chopped (optional)

THE TRADITIONAL WAY TO SOFTEN CORN TORTILLAS

Heat 1" corn oil or lard in a skillet over medium heat until the fat is hot enough that a drop of water splatters when dropped in the oil. Holding a tortilla with tongs, immerse it in the oil, turning it over a few times, until it becomes pliable. Drain on paper towels.

Chicken and Almond Fried Rice

SERVES 4

1. Heat the rice pouch in the microwave according to package directions.
2. Remove the skin and meat from the chicken; discard the skin and reserve the breast meat for another use. Shred the remaining meat.
3. Add the oil to a wok or large skillet and bring it to temperature over medium-high heat. Add the onions; stir-fry 1 minute. Add the rice and stir-fry 3 minutes. Stir in the shredded chicken, peas, and stir-fry sauce; stir-fry 3 more minutes or until heated through.
4. Add toasted sesame oil, soy sauce, and honey to taste if desired. Sprinkle with the almonds and serve.

1 (8.8-ounce) microwaveable pouch brown or white rice
1 (3-pound) rotisserie chicken
1 tablespoon peanut or vegetable oil
2 green onions, sliced
½ cup frozen peas
¼ cup bottled stir-fry sauce
Toasted sesame oil to taste (optional)
Soy sauce to taste (optional)
Honey to taste (optional)
¼ cup sliced almonds

Chicken Tetrazzini

SERVES 8

1. Preheat oven to 350°F.
2. Remove and discard the skin from the chicken; remove the meat from the bones and shred it.
3. In a large ovenproof Dutch oven, cook the spaghetti according to package directions. Add the asparagus during the last minute of cooking. Drain; set aside and keep warm.
4. Wipe out the Dutch oven; add the butter and melt it over medium heat. Add the mushrooms and peppers; sauté 8 minutes or until the mushrooms are tender. Stir in the flour and black pepper until well combined. Whisk in the broth and milk; cook, stirring frequently, until thickened and bubbly. Add the cooked pasta, asparagus, chicken, Swiss cheese, and half of the lemon peel; toss gently to coat.
5. In a medium bowl, toss together the bread cubes, olive oil, and remaining lemon peel; spread on top of the pasta mixture. Bake uncovered 15 minutes or until the bread cubes are golden brown. Let stand 5 minutes before serving. Garnish with parsley before serving.

1 (3-pound) roasted chicken
8 ounces dried spaghetti or linguini, broken in half
12 ounces fresh asparagus, trimmed and cut into 1" pieces
2 tablespoons butter
8 ounces small button or cremini mushrooms, sliced
1 large red bell pepper, seeded and cut into 1" pieces
1 large yellow bell pepper, seeded and cut into 1" pieces
¼ cup all-purpose flour
⅛ teaspoon freshly ground black pepper
1 (14-ounce) can chicken broth
¾ cup whole milk
2 ounces Swiss cheese, grated
1 tablespoon finely shredded lemon peel, divided
1½ cups bread cubes
1 tablespoon extra-virgin olive oil
2 tablespoons chopped fresh parsley

BREAD CUBES WISDOM

One thick-cut slice of bread will make about ¾ cup of bread cubes. Keep in mind that the cubes will only be as good as the bread you use to make them. Sourdough bread works well in the Chicken Tetrazzini recipe.

Chicken and Vegetables in Hoisin Sauce

SERVES 4

1. Heat the rice pouch in the microwave according to package directions.
2. Remove and discard the skin from the chicken. Remove the breast meat; wrap and refrigerate it for a later use. Remove the remaining meat from the bones and shred it.
3. Add the bell pepper, onion, garlic, salt, pepper, orange juice, and hoisin to a large microwave-safe bowl; stir to mix. Cover and microwave on high 1 minute; stir and microwave at 70 percent power 1 minute or until the pepper and onion are tender.
4. Stir in the cooked rice and shredded chicken; cover and microwave at 70 percent power 2 minutes or until the entire mixture is heated through. Serve garnished with kumquats, green onions, and/or toasted almonds if desired.

1 (8.8-ounce) microwaveable pouch brown or white rice
1 (3-pound) rotisserie chicken
1 medium red bell pepper, seeded and cut into thin strips
1 small yellow onion, peeled and cut into thin wedges
1 clove garlic, minced
Salt to taste
1/8 teaspoon freshly ground black pepper
2 tablespoons orange juice
2 tablespoons hoisin sauce
Sliced kumquats to taste (optional)
Sliced green onions to taste (optional)
Toasted sliced almonds to taste (optional)

Hot Chicken Fajita Pasta Salad

SERVES 6

1. Remove and discard the skin from the chicken; remove the meat from the bones and shred it. Set aside.
2. In a Dutch oven, cook the pasta according to the package directions; drain and keep warm. Wipe out the Dutch oven, add the oil, and bring it to temperature over medium heat. Add the onion, bell pepper, and Anaheim pepper; sauté 5 minutes or until crisp-tender.
3. Add the sour cream, marinade, lime juice, chili powder, cumin, and red pepper flakes to a small bowl; stir to mix.
4. Add the cooked noodles, chicken, and sour cream mixture to the sautéed vegetables; toss to coat. Leave on the heat long enough to reheat the noodles and warm the chicken if necessary. Garnish with chopped cilantro if desired. Serve warm.

1 (3-pound) rotisserie chicken
12 ounces dried egg noodles
2 tablespoons extra-virgin olive oil
1 medium yellow onion, peeled, halved, and thinly sliced
1 medium red bell pepper, seeded and cut into thin strips
1 Anaheim chili pepper, seeded and cut into thin strips
8 ounces sour cream
½ cup chipotle liquid meat marinade
2 tablespoons lime juice
1 teaspoon chili powder
1 teaspoon ground cumin
½ teaspoon dried red pepper flakes, crushed
Chopped fresh cilantro to taste (optional)

HEAT HINTS

The dried red pepper flakes and Anaheim chili pepper will add heat to this dish, which will be somewhat tempered by the cooked noodles and sour cream. If you prefer a milder taste, reduce the amount you add at first, taste the salad, and then add more, if needed.

Indian Chicken Vindaloo

SERVES 4–8

1. Bring the ghee to temperature over medium heat in a 6-quart Dutch oven. Fry the chicken pieces until browned, about 5 minutes on each side. Remove the chicken from the pan and keep warm.
2. Add the garlic and onion to the pan and sauté until golden brown. Stir in the ginger, cumin, mustard seeds, cinnamon, cloves, turmeric, cayenne, and paprika; sauté 2–3 minutes.
3. Stir in the tamarind paste, lemon juice, vinegar, brown sugar, salt, and water. Add the chicken pieces. Bring to a boil; cover, lower the heat, and simmer 45 minutes or until chicken is tender. Remove the cover and continue to simmer another 15 minutes or until the sauce thickens.

¼ cup ghee
8 bone-in chicken thighs, skin removed
3 cloves garlic, minced
2 large yellow onions, peeled and diced
2 tablespoons grated fresh ginger
2 teaspoons ground cumin
2 teaspoons yellow mustard seeds, crushed
1 teaspoon ground cinnamon
½ teaspoon ground cloves
1 tablespoon ground turmeric
1½ teaspoons cayenne pepper, or to taste
1 tablespoon paprika
1 tablespoon tamarind paste
2 teaspoons fresh lemon juice
2 tablespoons white vinegar
1 teaspoon light brown sugar
1–2 teaspoons salt
2 cups water

CUCUMBER SALAD WITH YOGURT

Chicken Vindaloo is wonderful served with a simple cucumber salad. Thinly slice 2 cucumbers; dress the slices with 2 tablespoons fresh lemon juice, ¼ cup extra-virgin olive oil, and salt and freshly ground black pepper to taste. Add a dollop of plain yogurt to each serving of the salad.

Honey-Mustard Barbecue Chicken Sandwiches

SERVES 8

1. Remove and discard the skin from the chicken; remove the meat from the bones and shred it.
2. Add the chicken to a nonstick saucepan or skillet along with the barbecue sauce, honey, mustard, and Worcestershire. Cook and stir over medium heat until heated through. Divide between the buns.

1 (3-pound) rotisserie chicken
1½ cups bottled barbecue sauce
¼ cup honey
2 teaspoons yellow mustard
1½ teaspoons Worcestershire sauce
8 sesame seed hamburger buns

Moroccan Chicken and Vegetables

SERVES 4-8

1. Add the oil to a 6- or 8-quart Dutch oven; bring to temperature over medium-high heat. Add the chicken pieces and brown on both sides. Remove from the pan and keep warm.
2. Reduce heat to low and add the onion, garlic, and eggplant. Sauté 5–10 minutes or until the onion is transparent. Increase the heat to medium-high; stir in the broth, cinnamon sticks, curry powder, cumin, turmeric, and black pepper and bring to a boil. Reduce heat and simmer 10 minutes.
3. Add the chicken, carrots, zucchini, turnip, and red pepper. Cover and simmer 10 minutes. Add the tomato, raisins, and half of the cilantro; cover and simmer 10 minutes or until the chicken is cooked through.
4. Taste for seasoning and add more salt and pepper, if necessary. Garnish with the remaining cilantro.

3 tablespoons extra-virgin olive oil
4 chicken thighs, skin removed
2 boneless chicken breasts, halved and skin removed
1 large yellow onion, peeled and diced
3 cloves garlic, minced
1 large eggplant, diced
3 cups chicken broth
2 (2") cinnamon sticks
1 teaspoon curry powder
1 teaspoon ground cumin
¼ teaspoon ground turmeric
¼ teaspoon freshly ground black pepper
2 large carrots, peeled and diced
1 large zucchini, diced
1 large white turnip, peeled and diced
1 small red bell pepper, seeded and diced
2 cups diced tomatoes
½ cup golden raisins
2 tablespoons chopped fresh cilantro, divided

EGGPLANT MATTERS

Some people find the taste of eggplant to be bitter unless it's first salted and allowed to sit 20 minutes. If you take that step, drain off any liquid after 20 minutes, then rinse the eggplant and let it drain well again.

Chicken and Stuffing Casserole

SERVES 4-6

1. Preheat oven to 350°F.
2. Melt the butter in a deep 3½-quart ovenproof nonstick skillet; add the onion and celery and sauté until softened, about 5 minutes.
3. Pour the sautéed vegetables into a large bowl and stir in the stuffing mix and its seasoning packet, if there is one. Add the broth or water and stir to combine; set aside to allow the liquid to be absorbed.
4. Spread the chicken cubes evenly in the bottom of the skillet. Mix the soup with the sour cream and spoon it evenly over chicken. Spread the green beans evenly over the soup mixture, and then sprinkle stuffing mixture evenly over all. Bake uncovered 45 minutes or until the chicken is cooked through. At the 30-minute mark, add the cheese if using, then bake an additional 15 minutes or until the cheese is melted.

⅓ cup butter
1 small yellow onion, peeled and chopped
2 stalks celery, chopped
1 (6–8-ounce) package of stuffing mix
1⅔ cups chicken broth or water
4 (4-ounce) boneless, skinless chicken breast halves, cut into 1" chunks
1 (10¾-ounce) can condensed cream of mushroom soup
⅓ cup sour cream
1 (14.5-ounce) can green beans, drained
1 cup grated Cheddar cheese (optional)

TOP IT OFF WITH DELICIOUSNESS

You can punch up the flavor of this dish by sprinkling a 2.8-ounce can of French-fried onions over the top before you bake it. If you want a fresher taste, you can make your own by sautéing thin strips of onions in vegetable oil until they are crispy, about 3 minutes.

Chicken Simmered with Olives

SERVES 4

1. Add the oil to a deep 3½-quart nonstick skillet and bring to temperature over medium heat. Brown the chicken, frying it about 5 minutes on each side. Remove the chicken from the pan and keep warm.
2. Add the onions and sauté until transparent, about 5–7 minutes. Add the garlic, ginger, turmeric, paprika, salt, and pepper; stir into the onions and sauté 1 minute.
3. Add the chicken back to the pan; pour the tomatoes over the chicken and sprinkle the lemon over the tomatoes. Cover, reduce heat, and simmer 30 minutes or until the chicken is tender.
4. Sprinkle the parsley, coriander, and olives over the top; cover and cook an additional 5 minutes. Serve warm over cooked couscous or rice.

2 tablespoons extra-virgin olive oil
8 small chicken thighs
1 large yellow onion, peeled and diced
3 cloves garlic, minced
1 teaspoon ground ginger
½ teaspoon ground turmeric
½ teaspoon paprika
Salt to taste
½ teaspoon freshly ground black pepper
1 (15-ounce) can diced tomatoes
1 preserved lemon, rinsed and diced
1 teaspoon dried parsley
1 teaspoon ground coriander
1 (7.5-ounce) jar pimiento-stuffed olives, drained
2 cups cooked couscous or rice

PRESERVED LEMONS

To make preserved lemons, cut 5 lemons into partial quarters, leaving them attached at one end; rub kosher salt over the outside and cut sides of the lemons, and then pack them tightly in a sterilized 1-quart glass jar. Add 2 tablespoons kosher salt and enough lemon juice to cover the lemons. Seal and let set at room temperature for 14 days, inverting the jar once a day to mix. Store indefinitely in the refrigerator.

Puerto Rican Chicken and Beans

SERVES 8

1. Add the salt pork or bacon to a large Dutch oven; cook over medium heat until the fat is rendered from the bacon. Add the carrot and celery; sauté 3–5 minutes or until soft. Add the onion and sauté until transparent, about 5 minutes. Add the garlic and sauté an additional 30 seconds.
2. Stir in the sausage; continue to stir while it fries for a few minutes, then stir in the ham. Add the chicken to the pan, skin-side down, pushing the other ingredients to the side so that as much of the chicken as possible touches the pan bottom. Cover and cook 10 minutes.
3. Add the water, Worcestershire, and hot sauce and bring to a simmer; reduce heat, cover, and simmer 35–45 minutes or until the chicken is cooked through. Remove the chicken from the pan and set aside.
4. Add the potatoes, cabbage, kale, and turnips to the pan. Stir to combine with the other ingredients. Cover and simmer 30 minutes.
5. Shred the chicken, discarding the skin and bones. Stir the shredded chicken into the pan.
6. Stir the beans into the pan. Add additional water if needed to prevent the pan from boiling dry. Cover and simmer 10 minutes. Add salt and pepper to taste.

¼ pound salt pork or bacon, diced
1 large carrot, peeled and shredded
1 stalk celery, finely diced
1 large yellow onion, peeled and diced
3 cloves garlic, minced
½ pound chorizo sausage, diced or thinly sliced
½ pound ham, chopped
8 bone-in, skin-on chicken thighs
4 cups water, or more, as needed
2 teaspoons Worcestershire sauce
Hot sauce to taste
4 large russet potatoes, peeled and diced
1 small head green cabbage, cored and thinly sliced
2 cups thinly sliced kale (tough stems removed)
4 medium turnips, peeled and diced
1 (15-ounce) can white beans, rinsed and drained
Salt to taste
Freshly ground black pepper to taste

Traditional Turkey Casserole

SERVES 8

1. Preheat oven to 350°F.
2. Add the oil and butter to an ovenproof Dutch oven and bring it to temperature over medium heat. Add the onion, green pepper, carrot, celery, salt, and pepper and sauté until tender, about 10 minutes.
3. Add the turkey and lightly sauté it with the vegetables to bring it to temperature. Stir in the mayonnaise, soups, eggs, and milk; mix well. Add the bread pieces and half of the grated cheese; toss to combine.
4. Cover and bake 45 minutes. Remove the lid and top with the remaining cheese. Bake an additional 15 minutes or until the cheese is melted and the casserole is cooked through. Serve immediately.

1 tablespoon extra-virgin olive oil
1 tablespoon butter
1 large yellow onion, peeled and finely chopped
1 medium green bell pepper, finely chopped
1 large carrot, peeled and finely chopped
1½ cups finely chopped celery
½ teaspoon salt
¼ teaspoon freshly ground black pepper
2 cups chopped cooked turkey
½ cup mayonnaise
1 (10¾-ounce) can condensed cream of mushroom soup
1 (10¾-ounce) can condensed cream of celery soup
4 large eggs, beaten
3 cups whole milk
1 loaf white bread, torn into small pieces
1 pound Cheddar cheese, grated

A TURKEY CASSEROLE TWEAK

Add a turkey stuffing taste to your casserole by adding 1 teaspoon poultry seasoning, dried sage, or a ½ teaspoon dried marjoram and ½ teaspoon dried thyme.

Mock Bratwurst in Beer

SERVES 8

1. Add all the ingredients to a 4-quart slow cooker in the order given. Note that the liquid amount needed will depend on how wet the sauerkraut is when you add it. The liquid should come up halfway and cover the turkey breast, with the sauerkraut and potatoes being above the liquid line. Add more beer if necessary.
2. Cook on low 6–8 hours. Serve hot.

2 stalks celery, finely chopped
1 (1-pound) bag baby carrots
1 large yellow onion, peeled and sliced
2 cloves garlic, minced
2–4 slices bacon, cut into small pieces
2 pounds turkey breast
1 (2-pound) bag sauerkraut, rinsed and drained
8 medium red potatoes, pierced
1 (12-ounce) can beer
1 tablespoon Bavarian seasoning
Salt to taste
Freshly ground black pepper to taste

BAVARIAN SEASONING

The Spice House (www.thespicehouse.com) has a salt-free Bavarian seasoning blend that is appropriate for this recipe. It's a blend of Bavarian-style crushed brown mustard seeds, French rosemary, garlic, Dalmatian sage, French thyme, and bay leaves.

Bavarian-Style Turkey Sausage Skillet

SERVES 6

1. Add the oil to a deep 3½-quart nonstick skillet or electric skillet and bring it to temperature over medium-high heat. Add the onions and sauté about 8 minutes or until tender. Sprinkle the flour over the onions and cook 2 minutes, stirring frequently.

2. Slowly whisk in the apple cider, broth, and mustard. Bring to a boil while you continue to stir, then add the potatoes, sausage, sauerkraut, brown sugar, and caraway seeds. Reduce heat and cover the pan; simmer about 30 minutes or until the sauce is thickened and the potatoes are tender. If desired, stir cranberries or raisins into the sausage mixture. Serve immediately.

1 tablespoon cooking oil
1 medium yellow onion, peeled and sliced
2 tablespoons all-purpose flour
1 cup apple cider or apple juice
½ cup chicken broth
2 tablespoons stone-ground mustard
1 (20-ounce) package refrigerated red potato wedges
1 pound cooked smoked turkey sausage, cut into bite-sized slices
1 (14.5-ounce) can sauerkraut, rinsed and drained
2 packed tablespoons light brown sugar
½ teaspoon caraway seeds
¼ cup dried cranberries or raisins (optional)

Turkey Pilaf

SERVES 4-6

1. Add the butter to a Dutch oven or 4-quart nonstick saucepan and melt over medium heat. Add the onion or shallot, if using, and sauté 2 minutes. Add the rice and brown it in the butter. Add the garlic and sauté 30 seconds. Pour in the broth and wine. Bring to a boil and then add the salt. Cover and simmer 20 minutes or until the rice is tender.
2. While the rice cooks, microwave the vegetables in the bag 4–5 minutes.
3. Uncover the rice and add the turkey and vegetables. Stir to combine. Cover and cook on low 2 minutes. Remove the cover and stir. Cover and continue to cook until the turkey is warmed through if necessary.
4. Serve warm topped with the cheese.

2 tablespoons butter
1 small yellow onion or large shallot, peeled and chopped (optional)
1 cup uncooked long-grain rice
2 cloves garlic, minced
1½ cups chicken broth
½ cup dry white wine
Salt to taste
1 (12-ounce) package steam-in-the-bag frozen mixed vegetables
1–2 cups chopped cooked turkey
Freshly grated Parmigiano-Reggiano cheese to taste

VEGGIES FRESH FROM THE GARDEN PILAF

This recipe variation will require a second pot, but you can cut up a pound of fresh zucchini, yellow summer squash, and/or sweet peppers and sauté them in butter until tender. Substitute them for the microwave-steamed vegetables in step 3.

Turkey and Biscuits

SERVES 4

1. Preheat oven to 425°F.
2. Bring the oil and butter to temperature in a medium oven-proof Dutch oven over medium heat. Add the onion and celery and sauté 5 minutes or until the onion is transparent. Sprinkle the salt and flour over the cooked vegetables and stir-fry 2 minutes to cook the flour.
3. Slowly add the broth to the pan, whisking to prevent lumps from forming. Stir the milk into the broth. Increase the temperature to medium-high and bring to a boil. Reduce heat and simmer 5 minutes or until mixture begins to thicken. Add the peas and carrots, turkey, and pepper. Mix well.
4. Arrange the biscuits over the top of the turkey mixture. Bake 20–25 minutes or until the biscuits are golden brown.

1 tablespoon extra-virgin olive oil
1 tablespoon butter
1 medium yellow onion, peeled and chopped
1 stalk celery, chopped
Salt to taste
3 tablespoons all-purpose flour
1 cup chicken broth
1½ cups whole milk
1 (12-ounce) package frozen peas and carrots
2 cups cubed cooked turkey
Freshly ground black pepper to taste
1 (7.5-ounce) can refrigerator biscuits

GROUND TURKEY AND BISCUITS

You can substitute 1 pound ground turkey for the cooked turkey in this recipe. Simply add it when you sauté the onion and celery. Fry it until the turkey is cooked through, using a spatula to break up the turkey as it cooks. You may need to drain off a little excess oil before you add the flour, but otherwise you simply follow the recipe.

Cranberry Turkey Quesadilla

SERVES 1

1. Pour the oil into a small nonstick skillet. Add 1 tortilla and coat one side with oil. Remove and repeat with the second tortilla.
2. Mix together the cranberry sauce, salsa, cheese, turkey, and jalapeño (if using) in a medium bowl. Spread the mixture over the tortilla in the pan. Top with the other tortilla, oiled side up. Press gently but firmly to keep the quesadilla together.
3. Place the pan over medium heat. Cook about 2 minutes or until the bottom is lightly browned. Flip the quesadilla and cook another 2 minutes or until that side is lightly browned and the cheese is melted.

2 teaspoons extra-virgin olive oil
2 (8") flour tortillas
1 tablespoon cranberry sauce
1 tablespoon salsa
½ cup grated Monterey jack or Cheddar cheese
¼ cup chopped cooked turkey
1 teaspoon chopped jalapeño pepper (optional)

Turkey and Cashew Stir-Fry

SERVES 4

1. Heat the rice pouch in the microwave according to the package directions.
2. Add the oil to a wok or large, deep skillet. Bring to temperature over medium-high heat. Add the vegetables and stir-fry 3–5 minutes for fresh vegetables or 7–8 minutes for unthawed frozen vegetables, or until crisp-tender.
3. Stir in the turkey and cook until it is warmed through. Add the stir-fry sauce and stir it in with the turkey-vegetable mix. Cook until the sauce is heated through. Add the cooked rice and toss gently to combine. Sprinkle with cashews and serve immediately.

1 (8.8-ounce) microwaveable pouch brown rice
1 tablespoon peanut oil
1 (16-ounce) package fresh-cut or frozen stir-fry vegetables (such as broccoli, pea pods, carrots, and water chestnuts)
1–2 cups chopped cooked turkey
¾ cup stir-fry sauce
½ cup chopped dry-roasted cashews

Oven-Roasted Turkey Breast with Asparagus

SERVES 4

1. Preheat oven to 325°F.
2. Place the potatoes on a microwave-safe plate and microwave on high 6–10 minutes or until they can be pierced easily with a knife.
3. In a small bowl, combine the butter, mustard, peppers, onion or shallot, tarragon, parsley, salt, and black pepper; set aside.
4. Carefully cut the potatoes into quarters. Add the potatoes, asparagus, and olive oil to a large resealable plastic bag. Close the bag and shake to coat the vegetables. Pour the potatoes and asparagus out of the bag into a 9" × 13" nonstick baking pan. Sprinkle salt and pepper to taste over the top.
5. Evenly spread the butter mixture over the top of the turkey cutlets. Place the cutlets on top of the potatoes and asparagus. Bake 15–20 minutes or until the turkey is baked through and the asparagus is tender.

4 medium baking potatoes, pierced
2 tablespoons butter, softened
1 teaspoon Dijon mustard
1 (7-ounce) jar roasted red sweet peppers, drained and chopped
4 teaspoons peeled and finely chopped red onion or shallot
¼ teaspoon dried tarragon, crushed
½ teaspoon dried parsley, crushed
⅛ teaspoon salt, plus more to taste
⅛ teaspoon freshly ground black pepper, plus more to taste
1 pound asparagus spears, woody ends removed
2 tablespoons extra-virgin olive oil
4 (4-ounce) boneless turkey breast cutlets

PAMPERING PICKY EATERS

If you have someone in your family who doesn't want one food to touch another, you can bake this recipe in 3 separate baking dishes. Treat them with nonstick spray and put the turkey cutlets in one, the potatoes in another, and the asparagus in the third. It defeats the one pot concept, but it will probably keep your life simpler.

Thai Turkey and Slaw

SERVES 4

1. In a large skillet, stir together green curry paste and wine. Stir over medium-high heat 1–2 minutes or until most of the liquid is gone. Stir in the coconut milk and bring to a boil. Add the turkey. Reduce heat and continue to cook uncovered about 1–2 minutes or until the sauce thickens.
2. In a serving bowl, stir together the vinegar and sugar; whisk until the sugar dissolves. Add the green onions, cabbage, and cashews or peanuts to the bowl and toss to mix.
3. To serve, divide the turkey and sauce between 4 individual plates and serve the slaw on the side.

2–3 tablespoons Thai green curry paste
¼ cup dry white wine
½ cup unsweetened coconut milk
2 cups chopped cooked turkey
¼ cup rice or rice wine vinegar
½ teaspoon granulated sugar
6 green onions, cut into thin slivers lengthwise
2 cups finely shredded savoy cabbage, napa cabbage, bok choy, or gai choi
3 tablespoons chopped unsalted dry-roasted cashews or dry-roasted peanuts

MAKING A COCONUT MILK SUBSTITUTE

If you don't have coconut milk on hand, make a good substitute by mixing unsweetened flaked coconut with an equal amount of milk and simmering the mixture 2 minutes or until it begins to foam; strain and use in any recipe that calls for coconut milk.

Turkey and Gruyère Noodle Casserole

SERVES 8

1. Cook the noodles in a large Dutch oven according to package directions. Drain, set aside, and keep warm.
2. Preheat oven to 350°F.
3. Wipe out the Dutch oven. Add the oil and bring it to temperature over medium-high heat. Add the bacon and cook 3 minutes to render the bacon fat and until the bacon begins to brown at the edges. Add the ground turkey; brown the turkey, crumbling it apart. Add the mushrooms and onions; stir-fry 3–5 minutes or until the onions are transparent and the meat loses its pink color. Sprinkle with the salt, pepper, and thyme.
4. Stir in the wine, deglazing the pan by scraping up any food stuck to the bottom of the pan. Stir in the broth and bring to a boil; boil 2 minutes, stirring occasionally.
5. Lower the heat to a simmer and whisk in the cream. Stir in the nutmeg and cheese. Stir in the noodles. Top with the bread crumbs; drizzle the butter over the crumbs. Bake 30 minutes or until the crumbs are browned.

1 pound dried extra-wide egg noodles
1 tablespoon extra-virgin olive oil
6 slices bacon or turkey bacon, chopped
2½ pounds ground turkey
1 pound white mushrooms, sliced
1 large yellow onion, peeled and diced
Salt to taste
Freshly ground black pepper to taste
1 tablespoon dried thyme
1 cup dry white wine
2 cups chicken broth
1 cup heavy cream
¼ teaspoon freshly grated nutmeg
8 ounces Gruyère cheese, grated
1 cup plain bread crumbs
2 tablespoons butter, melted

Stovetop Moroccan Turkey Casserole

SERVES 6

1. Bring the oil to temperature over medium heat in a large Dutch oven. Add the carrots; sauté 3 minutes. Add the onions; sauté 3 minutes. Stir in the garlic, cumin, paprika, turmeric, cinnamon, and cayenne; sauté 30 seconds. Stir in 1 cup of the broth and bring to a boil. Stir in the couscous and dates. Remove from heat, cover, and let stand 5 minutes or until the liquid is absorbed.

2. Stir the remaining 1 cup broth into the couscous mixture. Return to heat and bring to a boil. Stir in the turkey, spinach, and cereal. Reduce heat, cover, and simmer 3 minutes or until the turkey is heated through and the cereal has absorbed the extra broth. Serve immediately.

1 tablespoon vegetable oil
2 cups baby carrots, halved lengthwise
6 green onions, diced
3 cloves garlic, minced
1 teaspoon ground cumin
1 teaspoon paprika
1/2 teaspoon ground turmeric
1/4 teaspoon ground cinnamon
1/8 teaspoon cayenne pepper
2 cups chicken broth, divided
2/3 cup quick-cooking couscous
6 pitted dates, quartered
3 cups cubed cooked turkey
2 cups torn fresh spinach
1 1/4 cups bran flakes cereal

Turkey "Lasagna"

SERVES 8

1. Preheat oven to 375°F.
2. Cook the lasagna noodles in a large Dutch oven according to the package directions until almost tender. Drain the noodles in a colander and rinse in cold water to stop the cooking. Drain well and set aside. Wipe out the Dutch oven.
3. In a small bowl, mix together the pesto and lemon peel; set aside.
4. Add the egg, ricotta, 1 cup mozzarella, and the salt and pepper to a medium bowl and mix well.
5. Lightly coat the Dutch oven with nonstick cooking spray. Arrange 4 cooked noodles in the bottom of the pan, trimming and overlapping them to cover the bottom of pan.
6. Top with the spinach. Sprinkle with half of the walnuts. Spread half of the ricotta cheese mixture evenly over walnuts. Spread half of the pesto mixture evenly over the ricotta, then sprinkle half of the turkey over the pesto. Pour half of the pasta sauce evenly over the turkey. Top with another layer of noodles. Top with the mushrooms and remaining walnuts. Spread the remaining ricotta cheese mixture over mushrooms and walnuts. Spread the remaining pesto mixture over the ricotta. Sprinkle the remaining turkey over the pesto, and then pour the rest of the pasta sauce over the turkey. Top with another layer of noodles.

12 dried whole-wheat or regular lasagna noodles

½ cup basil pesto

1 teaspoon grated lemon peel

1 large egg, beaten

1 (15-ounce) carton ricotta cheese

2 cups grated mozzarella cheese, divided

¼ teaspoon salt

¼ teaspoon freshly ground black pepper

Nonstick cooking spray

2 cups chopped fresh spinach

½ cup chopped walnuts, divided, toasted if desired

2 cups chopped cooked turkey

1 (24-ounce) bottle marinara or pasta sauce

8 ounces button or cremini mushrooms, thinly sliced

½ cup dry red wine

Fresh Italian flat-leaf parsley leaves (optional)

7. Pour the wine into the empty marinara sauce jar, screw on the lid, and shake to mix with any sauce remaining in the jar. Pour over the top layer of noodles.
8. Cover the pan and bake 45 minutes.
9. Remove the cover. Sprinkle the remaining mozzarella cheese over the top. Bake an additional 15–30 minutes or until the cheese is melted and bubbly and the lasagna is hot in the center. Remove from the oven and let sit 10 minutes and then garnish with parsley if desired. To serve, cut the lasagna into pizza slice–style wedges.

Turkey, Spinach, and Artichoke Casserole

SERVES 10-12

1. Preheat oven to 375°F.
2. Evenly spread the artichoke hearts across the bottom of a 9" × 13" nonstick baking pan. Top with the spinach and turkey.
3. Add the cream cheese, mayonnaise, butter or oil, and cream or milk to a food processor; process until smooth. Spread over the top of the turkey. Sprinkle with pepper, and then the cheese.
4. Bake uncovered 40 minutes or until the cheese is bubbly and the casserole is lightly browned on top. This dish can be assembled the night before and refrigerated; allow extra baking time if you move the casserole directly from the refrigerator to the oven.

1 (14-ounce) jar artichoke hearts, drained and chopped
3 (10-ounce) packages frozen chopped spinach, thawed and well drained
2 cups finely chopped cooked turkey
2 (8-ounce) packages cream cheese, cut into cubes
2 tablespoons mayonnaise
1/4 cup butter or extra-virgin olive oil
6 tablespoons heavy cream or whole milk
Freshly ground black pepper to taste
1/2 cup freshly grated Parmigiano-Reggiano or Romano cheese

TURKEY, SPINACH, AND ARTICHOKE FONDUE

Add all ingredients to a food processor and process until smooth. Put into an electric fondue pot set at medium-high heat; bring it to temperature, stirring frequently. Once it's heated through, reduce the setting to warm to hold the fondue. Serve with bread, crackers, or crudités.

CHAPTER 6

Pork Entrées

Cranberry Roast Pork with Sweet Potatoes

SERVES 6-8

1. Place the pork, fat-side up, in a 4-quart slow cooker. Salt and pepper to taste.
2. Combine the cranberries, onion, orange juice, cinnamon, and cloves in a bowl or large measuring cup; stir to mix and then pour over the pork roast. Arrange the sweet potatoes around the meat. Cover and cook on low 5½–6 hours.
3. To serve with a thickened sauce, transfer the meat and sweet potatoes to a serving platter. Cover and keep warm.
4. Skim the fat off of the pan juices, leaving about 2 cups of juice in the cooker. Bring to a boil on the high setting. Combine the cornstarch with the water in a small bowl. Whisk into the boiling juices. Reduce the temperature setting to low and continue to cook and stir an additional 2 minutes or until the sauce is thickened and bubbly.

1 (3-pound) pork butt roast
Salt to taste
Freshly ground black pepper to taste
1 (16-ounce) can sweetened whole cranberries
1 medium yellow onion, peeled and chopped
¾ cup orange juice
¼ teaspoon ground cinnamon
¼ teaspoon ground cloves
3 large sweet potatoes, peeled and quartered
1 tablespoon cornstarch (optional)
2 tablespoons cold water (optional)

PAMPER THE PORK

Many slow cooker recipes can be changed from cooking on low to cooking on high simply by dividing the cooking time in half. It's trickier with pork, especially when cooking with a sugar-based or fruit sauce. If the dish scorches, the whole taste will change; if you cook on high, monitor it carefully during the last hour of cooking.

Pork and Vegetables Sautéed with Apples

SERVES 4-6

1. Place the pork, soy sauce, sherry, and ginger in a resealable plastic bag. Shake to evenly coat the meat. Let marinate in the bag 15 minutes.

2. Add the oil to a wok or large, deep nonstick skillet and bring it to temperature over medium-high heat. Drain the marinade from the meat; add the meat to the skillet and sauté 3 minutes. Add the onion and continue to sauté another 3 minutes or until the meat is cooked through and the onion is transparent.

3. Add the apples and sauté until they begin to turn brown. Push the contents of the pan to the side and add the garlic; sauté the garlic 30 seconds before stirring it into the meat mixture.

4. While the meat and apples are cooking, microwave the stir-fry vegetables according to the package directions for crisp-tender. Drain off any liquid from the vegetables. Add the vegetables, toasted sesame oil (if using), and pepper to the pan and toss with the meat mixture. Garnish with the green onion.

2 pounds pork steak, deboned and cut into thin strips
2 tablespoons soy sauce
2 tablespoons dry sherry
¼ teaspoon freshly grated ginger
3 tablespoons peanut oil
1 large yellow onion, peeled and diced
3 Golden Delicious apples, peeled and thinly sliced
4 cloves garlic, thinly sliced
1 (12-ounce) package steam-in-the-bag stir-fry mixed vegetables
1 teaspoon toasted sesame oil (optional)
Freshly ground black pepper to taste
4 green onions, chopped

Pork-Stuffed Acorn Squash

SERVES 8

1. Preheat oven to 350°F. Treat a roasting pan with nonstick spray.
2. Place the squash halves skin-side down in the roasting pan.
3. In a bowl, mix together the rice, peas, and sausage. Divide the mixture between the squash halves. Drizzle with the oil and season with salt and pepper to taste. Tightly cover the pan with heavy-duty foil. Bake 1 hour.
4. Remove the foil. Return the pan to the oven and bake another 15 minutes or until the squash is tender and the sausage is cooked through.

Nonstick cooking spray
4 acorn squash, halved and seeds removed
2 cups frozen brown rice
1 cup frozen peas
1 pound pork sausage
2 tablespoons extra-virgin olive oil, or to taste
Salt to taste
Freshly ground black pepper to taste

Milk-Baked Pork Tenderloin Meal

SERVES 4

1. Preheat oven to 350°F. Treat an 8" square Pyrex baking dish with nonstick spray.
2. Mix together the brown sugar, ginger, and mustard in a small bowl. Spread it over the meat. Lay the meat flat in the baking dish. Season with salt and pepper to taste. Pour the milk over the meat.
3. Rub each potato with 1 teaspoon butter or oil and wrap in individual pieces of aluminum foil. Place the potatoes in the dish with the meat. Bake 1½ hours or until all the liquid evaporates.

Nonstick cooking spray
2 teaspoons light brown sugar
1 teaspoon ground ginger
1 teaspoon ground mustard
4 (4-ounce) pork tenderloin cutlets, tenderized
Salt to taste
Freshly ground black pepper to taste
2 cups whole milk
4 large baking potatoes, pierced
4 teaspoons butter or extra-virgin olive oil, divided

Roast Pork Loin with Apples and Potatoes

SERVES 8

1. Preheat oven to 375°F.
2. Mix the salt, pepper, and herbes de Provence together and rub it into the meat. Add the butter and oil to a 9-quart Dutch oven, and bring to temperature over medium-high heat. Add the roast and brown it 2 minutes on all sides, or about 8 minutes.
3. Remove the meat from the pan and arrange the apple slices over the bottom of the pan. Sprinkle the apples with the sugar. Nestle the meat on top of the apples. Arrange the potato wedges around the meat. Season the potatoes with salt and pepper to taste.
4. Cover and bake 30 minutes. Remove the cover and baste the meat with the pan juices. Continue to bake uncovered 45 minutes or until the internal temperature of the roast is 150°F. Remove the roast to a serving platter and tent with aluminum foil; let rest 10 minutes.
5. Slice the pork crosswise into 8 slices. Arrange the apples and potatoes around the roast. Ladle the pan juices over the roast and serve immediately.

1 teaspoon kosher or sea salt, plus more to taste

¼ teaspoon freshly ground black pepper, plus more to taste

2 teaspoons herbes de Provence

1 (4-pound) pork loin, trimmed of fat and silver skin

2 tablespoons butter

1 tablespoon vegetable oil

3 large Golden Delicious apples, cored and cut into wedges

¼ teaspoon granulated sugar

4 large Yukon gold potatoes, peeled and quartered

PAN SIZE

The amount of air space between the food and the lid may add to the cooking time, but when in doubt, go bigger. It saves you the aggravation of having to move the ingredients to a bigger pot if the one you picked doesn't have enough room to hold all the ingredients, and it prevents boil-overs in the oven.

Pork Steaks in Plum Sauce

SERVES 4

1. At least 2 hours before you plan to cook the pork, put the prunes in a bowl and pour in the boiling water. Tightly cover with plastic wrap right away and set aside.
2. Before you begin cooking, drain the water from the prunes and mix them with the port (if using). Cover and allow the prunes to macerate.
3. Add the oil to a large nonstick skillet and bring to temperature over medium heat. Put the flour, salt, and pepper in a resealable plastic bag; shake to mix. Add the pork steaks to the bag; shake to coat the steaks in the flour. When the oil is hot, lay the steaks flat in the pan. Cook until the meat is almost cooked through and the floured surface forms a crust, about 15–20 minutes; turn the steaks and cook until done, about another 10–15 minutes. Place crust-side up on a serving platter; set in a warm oven to keep warm.
4. Add the shallots to the pan and sauté 30 seconds. Deglaze the pan with vinegar. Add the broth and bring to a gentle boil; cook about 5 minutes or until the liquid is reduced by half. Whisk in the jam and ketchup. Stir until the jam is melted. Arrange the prunes around the meat and pour the sauce over the top. Serve immediately.

12 pitted prunes
2 cups boiling water
$1/2$ cup port (optional)
3 tablespoons vegetable oil
2 tablespoons all-purpose flour
$1/2$ teaspoon salt
$1/4$ teaspoon freshly ground black pepper
4 (4-ounce) pork steaks
2 large shallots, peeled and minced
3 tablespoons red wine vinegar
$2/3$ cup beef broth
1 tablespoon plum jam
1 tablespoon ketchup

Beer-Baked Bratwurst

SERVES 4

1. Preheat oven to 425°F. Treat a large ovenproof Dutch oven with nonstick spray and lay the bratwurst in the pan. Bake uncovered 15 minutes.
2. Remove the pan from the oven and arrange the potatoes around the meat. Add the sauerkraut and onion over the potatoes and meat. Pour the beer into the pan, being careful that it doesn't foam up. Cover and bake 45 minutes.
3. Remove the cover and bake an additional 15 minutes or until the potatoes are tender and much of the beer has evaporated.
4. Serve the bratwurst with potatoes, sauerkraut, and some mustard on the side for dipping.

4 bratwurst
4 medium red potatoes, peeled and quartered
1 (2-pound) bag sauerkraut, rinsed and drained
1 large yellow onion, peeled and roughly chopped
1 (12-ounce) can beer, room temperature
Stone-ground or Bavarian-style mustard to taste

BAKED BRATWURST IN BEER FOR A CROWD

If you'll be serving the bratwurst for a casual meal with potato chips on the side, omit the potatoes. Add the desired amount of bratwurst and otherwise follow the baking instructions.

Ginger Pork and Vegetable Stir-Fry

SERVES 8

1. Put the pork steak strips in a resealable plastic bag along with 3 tablespoons of the soy sauce, the sherry or beer, and the ginger; seal and shake to mix. Marinate 15 minutes.
2. Add 1 tablespoon peanut oil to a wok and bring to temperature over medium-high heat. Sauté the pork 5 minutes or until cooked through. Remove the pork from the pan and keep warm.
3. Add the remaining tablespoon of peanut oil to the wok. Add the garlic, onion, and celery; sauté 3 minutes. Stir in the mushrooms, coleslaw mix, and bean sprouts. Sauté until the vegetables are crisp-tender. Stir the pork back into the vegetables.
4. In a small bowl, whisk together the remaining tablespoon of soy sauce, the chicken broth, sugar, and cornstarch. Add to the wok and stir until the mixture thickens and the cornstarch taste is cooked out of the liquids in the pan. Stir in the toasted sesame oil. Serve immediately.

3 boneless pork steaks, cut into thin strips
4 tablespoons soy sauce, divided
3 tablespoons dry sherry or beer
2 teaspoons grated fresh ginger
2 tablespoons peanut oil, divided
2 cloves garlic, minced
2 medium yellow onions, peeled and diced
6 stalks celery, chopped
8 ounces button mushrooms, sliced
3 cups coleslaw mix
2 cups bean sprouts
½ cup chicken broth
½ teaspoon granulated sugar
1 tablespoon cornstarch
½ tablespoon toasted sesame oil

Slow-Cooked Pork in Fruit Sauce

SERVES 6-8

1. Add the prunes, pork steaks, apple slices, wine or apple juice, and cream to a 4-quart slow cooker. Salt and pepper to taste. Cover and cook on low 6–8 hours. Remove the meat and fruit to a serving platter and keep warm.
2. Bring the liquid in the cooker to a boil over the high setting. Reduce the setting to low and simmer until the mixture is reduced by half and thickened.
3. Whisk in the jelly. Whisk in the butter 1 teaspoon at a time for a richer, glossier sauce if desired. Ladle the sauce over the meat or pour it into a heated gravy boat.

12 pitted prunes
3 pounds boneless pork steaks, trimmed of fat
2 Granny Smith apples, peeled, cored, and sliced
¾ cup dry white wine or apple juice
¾ cup heavy cream
Salt to taste
Freshly ground black pepper to taste
1 tablespoon red currant jelly
1 tablespoon butter (optional)

HOW ABOUT SOME POTATOES WITH THAT

To serve 8, wash 8 medium baking potatoes and pierce each twice with a knife. Arrange on a microwave-safe plate; microwave on high 10 minutes. Test for doneness; microwave longer if necessary. Wrap each potato in foil until it's time to serve them. Have butter and sour cream available at the table.

Mexican Pork Steak Burritos

SERVES 4

1. Add the oil to a nonstick skillet and bring to temperature over medium-high heat. Sauté the pork 2–3 minutes, and then add the garlic, onion, and red pepper. Continue to sauté until the onion is transparent and the pork is cooked through. Stir in the cumin, oregano, salt, black pepper, and cayenne or dried red pepper flakes (if using). Add the beer and cook until most of the moisture evaporates.
2. To fill the tortillas, spread refried beans on each tortilla. Top with the meat, shredded lettuce, sour cream, and green onion. Roll and eat like a burrito.

1–2 tablespoons peanut oil
1 pound boneless pork steak, cut into thin strips
2 cloves garlic, thinly sliced
1 small yellow onion, peeled and sliced
1 medium red bell pepper, seeded and diced
¼ teaspoon ground cumin
¼ teaspoon dried Mexican oregano
Salt to taste
Freshly ground black pepper to taste
Cayenne pepper or dried red pepper flakes to taste (optional)
2 tablespoons beer
4 flour or corn tortillas, heated
Refried beans, heated (optional)
Shredded lettuce (optional)
Sour cream (optional)
2 green onions, chopped (optional)

Slow-Cooked Pork Lo Mein

SERVES 6-8

1. Add the pork, onions, carrots, teriyaki glaze, celery, water chestnuts, bamboo shoots, and ginger to a 4-quart slow cooker. Cover and cook on low 7 hours.

2. Turn the cooker setting to high; add the peas and broccoli. Cover and cook 10–15 minutes or until the peas are crisp-tender.

3. Add the egg noodles and stir to mix. Reduce the setting to warm and cover; let steam 30 minutes or until the pasta is done. Serve immediately. Sprinkle cashews over each serving.

1½ pounds boneless pork shoulder, trimmed and cut into ¾" pieces

2 medium yellow onions, peeled and sliced

2 cups frozen sliced carrots

1 (12-ounce) jar teriyaki glaze

1 cup thinly bias-sliced celery

1 (8-ounce) can sliced water chestnuts, drained

1 (5-ounce) can sliced bamboo shoots, drained

1 teaspoon grated fresh ginger

1 (6-ounce) package frozen sugar snap peas

1 cup broccoli florets

8 ounces dried egg noodles

½ cup cashew halves

Filipino Pork with Rice Noodles

SERVES 6–8

1. Put the rice noodles in a bowl and pour tepid (105°F) water over them. Allow to soak while you prepare the rest of the dish.
2. Heat a wok over medium-high heat; add the oil, garlic, and pork. Stir-fry until the pork is done. Add the sausage, onion, and cabbage. Stir-fry 2–3 minutes, and then add the soy sauce, broth, fish sauce, leeks, and annatto oil. Stir-fry until the cabbage is tender.
3. Add the drained rice noodles; reduce heat to medium and stir-fry until the noodles are tender. Serve garnished with the chopped cilantro.

1 (8-ounce) package rice noodles
¼ cup peanut oil
2 cloves garlic, minced
½ pound pork tenderloin, cut into thin strips
½ pound sweet Chinese sausage, cut into thin slices
1 large yellow onion, peeled and diced
1 cup chopped napa cabbage
2 tablespoons soy sauce
1½ cups chicken broth
2 tablespoons fish sauce
¼ cup chopped leeks
1 tablespoon annatto oil
Chopped fresh cilantro to taste

Pork Chops with Roasted Red Peppers

SERVES 4

1. Bring the oil to temperature in a deep 3½-quart nonstick skillet or electric skillet over medium heat. Add the pork chops. Season the chops with salt and pepper to taste. Brown 5 minutes on each side. Remove from the pan and keep warm.
2. Add the potatoes and onion and sauté 5 minutes or until browned, stirring occasionally. Add the oregano and broth and stir to mix. Return the chops to the pan. Top with the red peppers and green beans. Bring to a boil and then reduce the heat, cover, and simmer 10 minutes or until done.

1 tablespoon extra-virgin olive oil
4 boneless pork chops, ½" thick
Salt to taste
Freshly ground black pepper to taste
4 medium red potatoes, peeled and diced
1 medium yellow onion, peeled and diced
1 teaspoon dried oregano, crushed
1 cup chicken broth
1 (4-ounce) jar roasted red peppers, drained and chopped
1 (12-ounce) bag frozen cut green beans

Braised Pork Roast with Kalamata Olives

SERVES 6

1. Add the oil to a large Dutch oven and bring it to the smoking point over medium-high heat. Add the pork and sear it on all sides until lightly browned, about 5 minutes on each side. Use tongs and a spatula to remove the meat.
2. Add the onion and sauté until transparent; stir in the garlic and sauté another 30 seconds. Add the bay leaves, and then deglaze the pan with the vinegar. Stir in the red wine and chicken stock.
3. Season the pork with salt and pepper and return it to the pan. Peel off a strip of skin around each potato and add them to the pan.
4. Cover and cook the pork and potatoes over low heat about 45 minutes, basting occasionally. Discard the bay leaves. Remove the meat to a platter; tent with foil and let it rest 20 minutes. Remove the potatoes and keep them warm.
5. Reheat the pan juices and add the olives, parsley, and thyme. Cut the strings around the roast to remove the rack of bones. Carve into 6 servings. Spoon the sauce over each rib and serve. Put extra sauce in a gravy boat for the table.

1 tablespoon macadamia nut or vegetable oil
1 (3½-pound) rack of pork, 6 ribs
1 medium red onion, peeled and chopped
5 cloves garlic, minced
3 bay leaves
½ cup red wine vinegar
½ cup red cooking wine
1 cup chicken stock
Salt to taste
Freshly ground white pepper to taste
6 medium red potatoes
¼ cup sliced kalamata olives
1 teaspoon dried parsley
1 teaspoon thyme, crushed

Three-Pork Pie

SERVES 8

1. Preheat oven to 375°F.
2. Add the butter and onion to a large microwave-safe bowl. Cover and microwave on high 1 minute. Stir to mix the melted butter with the onion. Break the sausage apart into the butter-onion mixture; stir to combine. Cover and microwave on high for three 1-minute segments, stirring between each minute. If the sausage has lost its pink color, continue to step 3; if it hasn't, cover and microwave on high 1 more minute.
3. Sprinkle the flour over the sausage mixture in the bowl, then stir to combine. Stir in the milk or heavy cream. Cover and microwave on high 1 minute. Whisk in the parsley, sage or thyme, savory, and black pepper until the mixture is smooth and there are no lumps. Stir in the canned pork and broth.
4. Cut the baby potatoes in the vegetable blend into quarters, if desired, and then stir the entire bag and the ham into the mixture.
5. Divide the pork mixture between two 9½" deep-dish pie pans. Top each filled pie plate with a pie crust. Cut vents into the crust. Place the pie pans side by side on a large sheet pan (a safety measure to catch any drippings should a pan boil over).
6. Bake 45 minutes or until the crust is golden brown. Remove from the oven and let cool 10 minutes, then cut and serve.

3 tablespoons butter
1 medium yellow onion, peeled and diced
½ pound bulk pork sausage
3 tablespoons all-purpose flour
¼ cup whole milk or heavy cream
1 tablespoon dried parsley
¼ teaspoon dried sage or thyme
¼ teaspoon savory
¼ teaspoon freshly ground black pepper
1 (28-ounce) can heat-and-serve pork
1 (14-ounce) bag baby potatoes and
   vegetables blend, thawed
1 cup cubed cooked ham
2 refrigerated peel-and-unroll-style pie
   crusts

Easy Welsh Pork Pie

SERVES 6

1. Preheat oven to 375°F.
2. Add the pork, onion, eggs, cayenne, sage, Worcestershire, salt, and pepper to a deep-dish pie pan. Mix well and spread out evenly in the pan. Bake 30 minutes. Drain off any excess fat.
3. Cover the meat mixture with the pie crust. Cut vents in the crust. Bake 45 minutes or until the crust is golden brown and flaky.

1½ pounds lean ground pork
1 medium yellow onion, peeled and diced
2 large eggs
Pinch cayenne pepper
¼ teaspoon dried sage
2 tablespoons Worcestershire sauce
Salt to taste
Freshly ground black pepper to taste
1 refrigerated peel-and-unroll-style pie crust

Sausage and Bacon with Beans

SERVES 6-8

1. Add the bacon and sausage to a 4-quart Dutch oven and fry over medium heat until some of the fat begins to render from the meat. Add the carrot and celery; sauté along with the meat, stirring occasionally. When the meat is cooked through, drain all but 1–2 tablespoons of the rendered oil.
2. Add the onion and sauté until transparent, about 5 minutes. Add the garlic and sauté 30 seconds.
3. Add the bay leaf, thyme, broth, and beans. Stir to combine. Bring to a boil and then lower the heat, cover, and simmer 15 minutes.
4. Discard the bay leaf and add salt and pepper to taste. Add a few drops of hot sauce to enhance the flavor if desired.

1 (8-ounce) package bacon, cut into pieces
8 ounces ground pork sausage
3 large carrots, peeled and finely chopped
2 stalks celery, finely chopped
1 large yellow onion, peeled and finely chopped
2 cloves garlic, minced
1 bay leaf
½ teaspoon dried thyme, crushed
3 cups chicken broth
2 (15-ounce) cans cannellini beans, rinsed and drained
Salt to taste
Freshly ground black pepper to taste
Hot sauce to taste (optional)

Three-Cheese Sausage and Polenta Gratin

SERVES 4

1. Preheat oven to 400°F.
2. Add the sausage to a 3- or 4-quart ovenproof nonstick skillet; brown over medium-high heat, breaking apart the sausage as it cooks.
3. When the sausage is cooked through, add the mushrooms, onion, and garlic. Lower the heat to medium and sauté until the onion is transparent, about 5–7 minutes. Drain off any excess oil and transfer to a bowl; mix with the pasta sauce.
4. Wipe out the pan and add the olive oil, turning the pan to evenly coat the bottom of the pan. Set the pan over low heat. Drain the liquid off of cornmeal mush; cut it into 1"-thick slices and arrange around the bottom of the pan. As the mush softens from the heat, spread it out evenly over the bottom of the pan to form a crust.
5. Spread the ricotta over the crust. Top the ricotta with the sausage mixture. Spread the remaining cheeses over the top. Bake uncovered 30 minutes or until the cheese is melted, bubbling, and lightly golden brown.
6. Remove from the oven and let stand 10 minutes before cutting into 4 wedges to serve. Garnish with fresh basil if desired.

12 ounces sweet or hot bulk Italian sausage
8 ounces button or cremini mushrooms, sliced
1 medium yellow onion, peeled and diced
2 cloves garlic, minced
2 cups tomato-basil pasta sauce
1 tablespoon extra-virgin olive oil
1 (24-ounce) package prepared cornmeal mush
1 cup ricotta cheese
1 cup shredded mozzarella or provolone cheese
½ cup finely shredded Asiago cheese
Chopped fresh basil to taste (optional)

Scalloped Potatoes with Ham

SERVES 8

1. Preheat oven to 350°F.
2. Generously butter the bottom of a 9" × 13" nonstick baking pan. Evenly spread ⅓ of the potatoes across the bottom of the pan and sprinkle lightly with salt and pepper. Evenly sprinkle ⅓ of the onion over the potatoes, 2 tablespoons of the flour over the onion, and dot the flour with 3 tablespoons of butter. Add 1 cup ham in an even layer, and top that with 1 cup cheese. Add another layer of potatoes, salt, pepper, onion, flour, butter, ham, and cheese. Top with the remaining potatoes.
3. Slowly pour the hot milk over the potatoes, adding enough milk to bring the liquid level to just below the top of the potatoes. Cover with foil and bake 1 hour.
4. Remove the foil, top with the remaining cheese, and bake an additional 15 minutes or until the potatoes are cooked through, the sauce is thickened, and the cheese is melted and bubbling.

6 tablespoons butter, plus more for greasing
8 large russet potatoes, peeled and very thinly sliced
Salt to taste
Freshly ground black pepper to taste
1 large yellow onion, peeled and diced
6 tablespoons all-purpose flour, divided
2 cups cubed cooked ham, divided
3 cups grated Cheddar cheese, divided
4 cups whole milk, or more as needed, heated to almost boiling

Ground Pork and Eggplant Casserole

SERVES 8

1. Preheat oven to 350°F.
2. Bring a large Dutch oven to temperature over medium-high heat. Add the pork and fry until done, breaking it apart as it cooks. Remove from the pan and keep warm.
3. Drain off and discard any pork fat from the pan; add the oil to the pan and bring to temperature over medium heat. Add the onion, celery, and green pepper; sauté until the onion is transparent, about 5 minutes.
4. Add the eggplant, garlic, thyme, parsley, and tomato sauce. Stir to combine. Cover and sauté 20 minutes or until the vegetables are tender, stirring often. Return the ground pork to the pan. Add the hot sauce (if using), Worcestershire, salt, pepper, and egg; stir to combine.
5. Sprinkle the bread crumbs over the top and drizzle with the melted butter. Bake 40 minutes or until the crumb topping is lightly browned and the casserole is hot in the center.

2 pounds lean ground pork
2 tablespoons peanut or extra-virgin olive oil
2 large yellow onions, peeled and chopped
3 stalks celery, chopped
1 medium green bell pepper, seeded and chopped
4 medium eggplants, cut into ½" dice
6 cloves garlic, chopped
⅛ teaspoon dried thyme, crushed
1 tablespoon freeze-dried parsley
3 tablespoons tomato paste
1 teaspoon hot sauce (optional)
2 teaspoons Worcestershire sauce
Salt to taste
Freshly ground black pepper to taste
1 large egg, beaten
½ cup bread crumbs
1 tablespoon butter, melted

WHY USE FRESHLY GROUND BLACK PEPPER?

Bottled ground black pepper contains anti-caking agents that can cause stomach upset for some people and can also change the flavor. Dishes also taste more peppery when you grind the pepper yourself.

CHAPTER 7

Beef Entrées

Slow Cooker
Beef Brisket with Apples

SERVES 6-8

Add all the ingredients to a 4-quart slow cooker. Add additional water to just cover the meat if needed. Cook on low 6 hours or until the meat is tender.

1 (3–4-pound) beef brisket
1 large yellow onion, peeled and quartered
2 large cloves garlic, chopped
4 large cloves garlic, left whole
1 (10-ounce) jar apple jelly
3 tablespoons Dijon mustard
Salt to taste
Freshly ground black pepper to taste
3/4 teaspoon curry powder
1/3 cup dry white wine
1 cup apple juice
1 cup water, or more as needed

EVEN BETTER THE NEXT DAY

Brisket will be more tender if you allow it to cool in the broth, so this is a good dish to make the day before you plan to serve it. To reheat it, bake it 45 minutes at 325°F.

Baked Apple Butter Steak with Sweet Potatoes

SERVES 4-6

1. Preheat oven to 375°F. Treat a 9" × 13" nonstick baking pan with nonstick spray. Pour the apple juice or water into the pan.
2. In a small bowl, mix together the apple butter, soy sauce, sherry, ginger, and onions. Put the steak in the center of the baking pan and spread the apple butter mixture over the top of the meat. Arrange the Brussels sprouts and sweet potatoes around the steak. Salt and pepper to taste.
3. Cover and bake 45 minutes or until steak reaches desired doneness and the potatoes are tender.
4. If you wish, uncover and put under the broiler for a couple of minutes to glaze the sauce on top of the meat.

Nonstick cooking spray
½ cup apple juice or water
¼ cup apple butter
2 tablespoons soy sauce
2 tablespoons dry sherry
½ teaspoon grated fresh ginger
2 green onions, finely chopped
1 (1½-pound) sirloin steak, thick-cut
1 (12-ounce) bag frozen Brussels sprouts, thawed
2 large sweet potatoes, peeled and diced
Salt to taste
Freshly ground black pepper to taste

Roast Beef and Arugula with Whole-Grain Spaghetti

SERVES 4

1. In a large saucepan, cook the pasta according to the package directions. Drain the pasta in a colander; transfer to a covered oven-safe bowl and keep warm in the oven.
2. Add the olive oil to the same saucepan and bring to temperature over medium heat. Add the onion, garlic, and red pepper flakes; sauté 5 minutes or until the onion is tender, stirring occasionally.
3. Add the beef, undrained tomatoes, red peppers, vinegar, salt, and pepper to the pan. Heat through. Add the hot pasta to the pan along with the arugula or spinach and parsley; toss to combine. Top with the cheese. Serve immediately.

4 ounces dried whole-grain or whole-wheat spaghetti
1 tablespoon extra-virgin olive oil
1 medium yellow onion, peeled and diced
4 cloves garlic, minced
1/4 teaspoon dried red pepper flakes
12 ounces cooked roast beef, cut into bite-sized pieces
1 (14.5-ounce) can diced tomatoes with Italian herbs
1 cup bottled roasted red sweet peppers, drained and coarsely chopped
1 tablespoon balsamic vinegar
Salt to taste
1/2 teaspoon freshly ground black pepper
2 cups fresh baby arugula or spinach leaves
1 tablespoon chopped fresh Italian flat-leaf parsley
1 ounce Romano cheese, grated or shaved

Slow-Roasted Sirloin and Root Vegetables

SERVES 8

1. Preheat oven to 200°F.
2. To ensure the roast cooks evenly, tie it into an even form using butcher's twine. Mix together the salt, pepper, garlic powder, onion powder, cumin, thyme, and paprika. Pat the seasoning mixture on all sides of the roast. Heat a medium roasting pan over medium-high heat. Add the oil and bring to temperature; place the roast in the pan and sear it 3 minutes on all sides, or until brown.
3. Arrange the turnips, parsnips, potatoes, carrots, and sprouts around the roast. Distribute the garlic and arrange the onion slices over the vegetables. Drizzle with olive oil and season with salt and pepper to taste.
4. Roast, basting occasionally with the pan juices, 3 hours or until an instant-read thermometer inserted in the center registers 130°F for rare. Remove to a serving platter; cover and let rest about 15 minutes.
5. Put the pan on the stovetop over two burners on medium-high heat. Add the wine and water. Bring to a boil, stirring to scrape up any browned bits from the bottom of the pan. Cook about 5 minutes or until reduced by half. To serve, thinly slice the roast across the grain. Serve drizzled with some of the pan juices.

1 (4-pound) beef sirloin tip roast
1 teaspoon kosher or sea salt, plus more to taste
½ teaspoon freshly ground black pepper, plus more to taste
1 teaspoon garlic powder
1 teaspoon onion powder
1 teaspoon ground cumin
1 teaspoon dried thyme leaves, crushed
½ teaspoon sweet paprika
2 tablespoons extra-virgin olive oil, plus more to taste
2 turnips, peeled and cut into 2" pieces
2 parsnips, peeled and cut into 2" pieces
4 large red potatoes, peeled and quartered
1 (1-pound) bag baby carrots
1 (12-ounce) package frozen Brussels sprouts
8 cloves garlic, halved lengthwise
2 large yellow onions, peeled and sliced
½ cup dry red wine
1 cup water

Pot Roast with Fruit Sauce

SERVES 8-10

1. In a small bowl, stir together the garlic, sage, salt, black pepper, and cayenne. Spread the garlic mixture over both sides of the meat.

2. Add the oil to a 6-quart Dutch oven and bring it to temperature over medium heat; add the roast and brown it on all sides. Drain off the fat. Pour the broth over the roast and add the onion. Increase the heat to medium-high and bring to a boil. Tightly cover and reduce heat; simmer 1½ hours.

3. Add the fruit and vegetables to the pan. Add some water to the pan if needed to cover all the ingredients. Increase heat to return it to boiling, cover, and reduce heat; simmer 30 minutes or until the parsnips, carrots, and apples are tender. With a slotted spoon, transfer the meat, fruit, and vegetables to a serving platter.

4. Skim the fat off the juices that remain in the pan. Add water if necessary to bring the pan juices to 1½ cups. Bring to a boil over medium-high heat.

5. In a small bowl, whisk together the cold water and flour until smooth. Slowly whisk the flour mixture into the boiling pan juices. Boil 1 minute, then reduce heat to medium and continue to cook and stir until thickened. Stir in the balsamic vinegar. Serve the gravy over the roast, vegetables, and fruit.

2 cloves garlic, minced
1 teaspoon dried sage, crushed
½ teaspoon salt
½ teaspoon freshly ground black pepper
⅛ teaspoon cayenne pepper
1 (3-pound) boneless beef chuck pot roast
2 tablespoons vegetable oil
1 cup beef broth
1 large yellow onion, peeled and quartered
1 cup pitted prunes, halved
2 large apples, peeled, cored, and cut into thick slices
1 pound parsnips, peeled and cut into ½" pieces
1 (1-pound) bag baby carrots
½ cup cold water
¼ cup all-purpose flour
1 tablespoon balsamic vinegar

OR FOR A SLIGHTLY DIFFERENT FLAVOR . . .

Rather than adding the balsamic vinegar at the end, stir several finely crushed ginger snaps into the pan juices before you add the flour mixture. Once it's thickened, stir a teaspoon of red wine vinegar into the gravy.

Roast Beef with Horseradish Potatoes

SERVES 6-8

1. In a small bowl, mix together the horseradish, oil, pepper, thyme, and salt. Rub half of the horseradish mixture onto the meat.
2. Add the seasoned roast, celery, wine, and broth to a 4-quart slow cooker. Cover and cook 1–2 hours on high or until the celery is limp.
3. Peel off a thin strip of the skin from around each potato. In a small bowl or a resealable plastic bag, mix the potatoes with the remaining horseradish sauce.
4. Discard the celery. Add more water if necessary to bring the liquid level up to just the top of the meat. Add the potatoes and carrots to the cooker. Cover and cook on low 4–6 hours or until the meat is tender and the vegetables are cooked through. Serve warm.
5. If you wish to thicken the pan juices, remove the meat and vegetables to a serving platter. Cover with aluminum foil and keep warm. Turn the slow cooker to the high setting and bring the juices to a boil. Mix together the flour and butter, and whisk it into the boiling pan juices, 1 teaspoon at a time.

⅓ cup prepared horseradish
2 tablespoons extra-virgin olive oil
1 teaspoon freshly ground black pepper
1 teaspoon dried thyme, crushed
½ teaspoon salt
1 (3-pound) boneless beef chuck roast, trimmed and cut into 2" cubes
2 stalks celery, halved
¼ cup dry white wine or beef broth
1¼ cups beef broth
2 pounds small red potatoes
Water, as needed (optional)
1 (1-pound) package baby carrots
2 tablespoons all-purpose flour (optional)
2 tablespoons butter (optional)

LUCK OF THE LEFTOVERS: HORSERADISH—HEARTY BEEF STEW

If you have leftovers, you can make a hearty beef stew by cutting the meat into bite-sized pieces and adding them to the thickened pan juices. Add 1–2 tablespoons ketchup or some hot sauce for an extra punch of flavor if desired. Reheat and serve with hard rolls, or serve over biscuits.

Herbed Pot Roast

SERVES 8

1. Add the celery, roast, salt, pepper, onion, garlic, broth, vinegar, and thyme to a 4-quart slow cooker. Cover and cook on low 6 hours.
2. Peel off a strip of the skin from around each potato. Add to the slow cooker along with the carrots. Cover and cook an additional 2 hours on low.
3. If you wish to thicken the pan juices to make gravy, use a slotted spoon to transfer the meat and vegetables to a serving platter; keep warm. Cut the meat and vegetables into slices or chunks for easier serving. Increase the temperature on the slow cooker to high and bring 1½ cups of the strained pan juices to a boil. In a small bowl, use a fork to blend together the butter and flour. Whisk the flour mixture into the boiling juices, 1 teaspoon at a time. Once you've added all the mixture, boil 1 minute and then reduce the setting to low. Stir and simmer 2–3 more minutes or until the mixture is thickened.

2 stalks celery, diced
1 (3-pound) boneless beef chuck roast
Salt to taste
Freshly ground black pepper to taste
2 large yellow onions, peeled and quartered
2 cloves garlic, minced
2 cups beef broth
¼ cup red wine vinegar
1 teaspoon dried thyme, crushed
8 medium potatoes
2 pounds carrots, peeled
¼ cup butter, softened (optional)
¼ cup all-purpose flour (optional)

TURN THIS INTO IRANIAN BEEF ROAST

In step 1, omit the thyme and add a small can of diced tomatoes, ⅓ cup chopped fresh cilantro, ¾ teaspoon freshly ground black pepper, ¾ teaspoon ground cumin, ½ teaspoon ground coriander, ¼ teaspoon ground cloves, and a pinch each of ground cardamom, ground nutmeg, and ground cinnamon. In step 2, substitute thawed frozen green beans for the carrots.

Slow-Cooked Steak and Mushrooms

SERVES 8

1. Trim the fat from the steak; cut the meat into 8 pieces. Add the oil to a 4-quart slow cooker and bring to temperature on the high setting. Add the meat and brown it while you prepare the remaining ingredients.
2. Combine the beef gravy and mushroom gravy mix. Remove the meat from the cooker and spread the onions over the bottom of the crock. Place the meat on top of the onions, and arrange the mushrooms over the top of the meat. Pour the gravy mixture over the top.
3. Set the temperature to low and cook 8–10 hours.

2 pounds boneless beef round steak, ¾" thick
1 tablespoon vegetable oil
1 (12-ounce) jar beef gravy
1 (1-ounce) package dry mushroom gravy mix
2 medium yellow onions, peeled and sliced
3 cups sliced button or cremini mushrooms

Corn Chip and Chili Casserole

SERVES 4-6

1. Preheat oven to 350°F.
2. Treat a 9" deep-dish pie pan with nonstick cooking spray. Spread 2 cups of the corn chips over the bottom of the pan. Distribute the onion and ½ cup of the cheese over the top of the corn chips, and then top them with the chili. Add the remaining corn chips and cheese over the top of the chili.
3. Bake 15–20 minutes or until the casserole is heated through and the cheese is melted.

Nonstick cooking spray
3 cups corn chips, divided
1 large yellow onion, peeled and chopped
1 cup grated American cheese, divided
1 (19-ounce) can chili con carne

Slow-Cooked Beef Stew with Parsnips and Raisins

SERVES 4-6

1. Add the oil to a 4-quart slow cooker and bring to temperature over high heat. Toss the meat in the flour. Add half of the meat to the slow cooker and sauté until brown; push the meat to the side and add remaining meat, stirring to coat all the meat in the hot oil. Wipe out any excess fat.
2. Add the carrots, parsnips, onion, tomatoes, broth, garlic, bay leaf, thyme, and pepper to the cooker; stir to combine. Reduce heat to low; cover and cook 8–10 hours.
3. Remove and discard the bay leaf. Stir in the olives and raisins. Serve warm.

2 tablespoons vegetable oil
2 tablespoons all-purpose flour
1 (1½-pound) beef chuck roast, cut into 1" cubes
1 (1-pound) bag baby carrots
2 large parsnips, peeled and sliced into ½" pieces
1 large yellow onion, peeled and roughly chopped
1 (14.5-ounce) can diced tomatoes, undrained
1 (14-ounce) can beef broth
2 cloves garlic, minced
1 bay leaf
1 teaspoon dried thyme, crushed
¼ teaspoon freshly ground black pepper
½ cup almond- or pimiento-stuffed green olives
⅓ cup golden raisins

Grilled Herbed Tenderloin with Vegetables

SERVES 4

1. In a small bowl, mix together the garlic, basil, thyme, rosemary, mint, oil, salt, and pepper. Coat both sides of the steaks and the cut side of the tomatoes with the mixture.
2. Evenly coat the asparagus with the remaining garlic-herb mixture. Divide the mixture among 4 pieces of aluminum foil and fold the foil over to make packets.
3. Heat the grill on medium. Add the asparagus packets to the back of the grill. Grill the steaks over direct medium heat 5 minutes. Turn the steaks and asparagus packets. Add the tomatoes to the grill, cut-side down. Grill until the steaks reach the desired doneness: another 2 minutes for medium rare or 3–4 minutes for medium.

2 cloves garlic, minced
1 tablespoon dried basil
2 teaspoons dried thyme
1 teaspoon dried rosemary
1 teaspoon dried mint leaves
2 tablespoons extra-virgin olive oil
½ teaspoon salt
½ teaspoon freshly ground black pepper
4 (4-ounce) beef tenderloin steaks, cut 1" thick
2 large yellow tomatoes, cut in half crosswise
1 pound asparagus spears, trimmed

ALTERNATIVE FRESH HERBS MARINADE

Add 2 cloves garlic, ¼ cup fresh basil, 2 tablespoons fresh thyme leaves, 1 tablespoon fresh rosemary, and 1 tablespoon fresh mint leaves to a food processor. Cover and process until the herbs are chopped. With the food processor running, add 2 tablespoons extra-virgin olive oil in a thin, steady stream. Scrape the sides of the bowl, and stir in salt and freshly ground black pepper to taste.

Upside-Down Beef Potpie

SERVES 4

1. Preheat oven to 350°F.
2. Add ¼ cup of the butter to a large microwave-safe bowl; microwave on high 30 seconds or until the butter is melted. Pour the butter into an 8" square baking dish.
3. Add the flour, cheese, sugar, baking powder, salt, and milk to the bowl; stir until blended. Pour into the baking dish.
4. Add the remaining 2 tablespoons butter, the onion, carrots, and celery to the bowl. Cover and microwave on high 1 minute; stir to combine the vegetables with the melted butter. Cover and microwave on high 1 more minute or until the onion is transparent. Stir in the beef, thawed peas and carrots, potatoes, gravy, and mustard and mayonnaise (if using).
5. Pour the beef mixture over the batter. Do not stir. Bake 1 hour or until the beef topping is bubbly.

¼ cup plus 2 tablespoons butter
1½ cups all-purpose flour
1 cup grated Cheddar cheese
2 teaspoons granulated sugar
2 teaspoons baking powder
½ teaspoon salt
1½ cups whole milk
1 medium yellow onion, peeled and diced
2 baby carrots, shredded
½ stalk celery, finely diced
2 cups shredded cooked beef
1 cup frozen peas and carrots, thawed
1 cup diced cooked potatoes
1 cup beef gravy
1 teaspoon Dijon mustard (optional)
2 teaspoons mayonnaise (optional)

Steak and Mushroom Pie

SERVES 4

1. Preheat oven to 375°F.
2. Add the bacon, butter, onion, and mushrooms to a large microwave-safe bowl. Cover and microwave on high 1 minute. Stir to mix the melted butter with the other ingredients. Cover and microwave on high for three 1-minute segments, stirring between each minute. If the bacon has lost its pink color, continue to step 3; if it hasn't, cover and microwave on high for another minute.
3. Add the garlic and sprinkle the flour over the mushroom mixture in the bowl, then stir to combine. Slowly stir in the wine. Cover and microwave on high 1 minute. Whisk in the parsley and seasoning blend until the mixture is smooth and without lumps. Slowly stir in the broth.
4. Cut the baby potatoes in the vegetable blend into quarters, if desired, then stir the entire bag and the beef into the mixture.
5. Pour the beef mixture into a 9½" deep-dish pie pan. Top the filled pie pan with the pie crust. Cut vents into the crust. Place the pie pan on a sheet pan (a safety measure to catch any drippings should the pan boil over). Bake 45 minutes or until the crust is golden brown. Remove from the oven and let sit 10 minutes, and then cut and serve.

4 slices bacon, cut into small dice
2 tablespoons butter
1 small yellow onion, peeled and diced
8 ounces button or cremini mushrooms, sliced
2 cloves garlic, minced
3 tablespoons all-purpose flour
½ cup Madeira wine
1 teaspoon dried parsley
1 teaspoon Mrs. Dash Original Blend
½ cup beef broth
½ (14-ounce) bag baby potatoes and vegetables blend, thawed
1 cup shredded cooked sirloin steak or roast beef
1 refrigerated peel-and-unroll-style pie crust

Chili Con Carne

SERVES 4-6

1. Bring the oil to temperature over medium heat in a medium Dutch oven. Add the hamburger, onion, chili powder, and cumin. When the meat is cooked and the onions are transparent, drain any excess fat from the pan.
2. Add the remaining ingredients and stir to combine. Lower the heat, cover, and simmer 1–2 hours, stirring occasionally.

2 tablespoons peanut oil
1 pound lean hamburger
1 large yellow onion, peeled and chopped
3 tablespoons chili powder
1 teaspoon ground cumin
3 cloves garlic, diced
1 tablespoon Worcestershire sauce
1 (28-ounce) can chopped tomatoes
1 large green bell pepper, seeded and chopped
1 (15-ounce) can kidney beans, rinsed and drained
Salt to taste
Freshly ground black pepper to taste
1 teaspoon granulated or light brown sugar (optional)

FIESTA CHILI BUFFET

Have bowls of these condiments lined up so that family and guests can top their chili: crushed corn chips, shredded Cheddar cheese, cooked rice, shredded lettuce, chopped green pepper, sliced black olives, chopped tomatoes, diced onion or chopped green onions, toasted pecans or chopped peanuts, shredded coconut, and salsa.

Apricot Barbecued Pot Roast

SERVES 8

1. Add the ketchup, preserves, brown sugar, vinegar, teriyaki or soy sauce, red pepper flakes, mustard, and pepper to a 1-gallon resealable plastic bag; close and squeeze to mix. Add the roast to the bag. Refrigerate overnight.

2. Add the water and the cooking rack or steamer basket to a 6-quart or larger pressure cooker. Place half of the onions on the rack or basket. Use a slotted spoon to remove the roast pieces from the marinade and place them on the onions; reserve the marinade. Cover the roast pieces with the remaining onions.

3. Lock the lid in place on the pressure cooker. Place over medium heat and bring to high pressure; maintain for 50 minutes, or 15 minutes per pound (keeping in mind that you reduce the weight of the roast when you trim off the fat). Turn off the heat and allow 15 minutes for the pressure to release naturally. Use the quick release to release any remaining pressure and then carefully remove the lid.

4. Strain the pan juices into a bowl and set aside. Separate the meat from the onions and return the meat to the pan. Purée the onions in a food processor or blender.

5. Pour the reserved marinade into the cooker and use 2 forks to pull the meat apart and mix it into the sauce. Bring to a simmer over medium heat. Stir in the onion.

6. Add ½ cup of the reserved pan juices (skimmed of fat) to the cooker and stir it into the meat and sauce. Reduce heat to low and simmer 15 minutes or until the mixture is thick enough to serve on sandwiches.

½ cup ketchup
½ cup apricot preserves
¼ cup dark brown sugar
¼ cup apple cider or white vinegar
½ cup teriyaki or soy sauce
Crushed red pepper flakes to taste
1 teaspoon dry mustard
¼ teaspoon freshly ground black pepper
1 (4-pound) boneless chuck roast or pork shoulder roast, trimmed and cut into 1" cubes
1½ cups water for beef; 2 cups water for pork
1 large sweet onion, peeled and sliced

Tzimmes

SERVES 8

1. Preheat oven to 475°F.
2. Place the brisket fatty side up on a rack in a large roasting pan. Salt and pepper to taste. Bake 25 minutes to brown the meat. Remove the meat, leaving it on the rack, and set aside.
3. Add the onion, celery, and parsley to the pan. Place the brisket directly on top of the vegetables. Add the broth, lemon juice, cloves, and cinnamon. Cover the pan, reduce the oven temperature to 300°F, and bake 2½ hours.
4. Take the pan out of the oven and remove the cover. Add the sweet potatoes, carrots, and prunes to the pan. Mix together the honey and vinegar and pour over the meat. Cover and return to the oven; bake an additional 1½ hours.
5. Remove from the oven, cover, and let rest 15 minutes before carving the meat. Serve with the vegetables and the sauce that has formed in the pan.
6. For a richer sauce, after you remove the meat and vegetables to a serving platter, whisk the butter into the pan juices 1 teaspoon at a time before spooning it over the dish.

1 (4-pound) beef brisket
Salt to taste
Freshly ground black pepper to taste
1 large yellow onion, peeled and chopped
2 stalks celery, chopped
¼ cup chopped fresh flat-leaf parsley
3 cups beef broth
3 tablespoons fresh lemon juice
3 whole cloves
1½" piece cinnamon stick
4 large sweet potatoes, peeled and quartered
1 (1-pound) bag baby carrots
1 (12-ounce) box pitted prunes
1 tablespoon honey
2 tablespoons white or white wine vinegar
2 tablespoons butter (optional)

Ground Beef–Stuffed Grape Leaves

SERVES 4-6

1. In a bowl, mix together the beef, rice, cinnamon, allspice, salt, and pepper.
2. Drain the grape leaves. Use any small leaves to line the bottom of a heavy saucepan or Dutch oven treated with nonstick spray. Lay each larger leaf on a flat surface, vein-side up; trim off any stem.
3. Spoon some of the beef mixture onto the center of each grape leaf. To form each roll, fold the stem end over the filling, then fold the sides over each other, and fold down the tip. Carefully place each roll, seam-side down, in the saucepan. Place the rolls close together in the pan to prevent them from unrolling while they cook. You may end up with several layers of rolls, depending on the size of the pan.
4. Place a plate over the rolls and then add enough water or broth to cover the plate. Bring to a boil over medium-high heat, then reduce the heat, cover, and simmer 30 minutes.
5. Add the lemon juice; cover and continue to simmer an additional 30 minutes. The stuffed grape leaves are done when they're tender when pierced with a fork. You can serve them warm, at room temperature, or cool.

1 pound lean ground beef
1 cup uncooked long-grain rice
¼ teaspoon ground cinnamon
¼ teaspoon ground allspice
Salt to taste
Freshly ground black pepper to taste
1 (1-pound) jar of grape leaves
Nonstick cooking spray
Water or chicken broth as needed
Juice of 2 large lemons

Reuben Casserole

SERVES 4-6

1. Preheat oven to 350°F. Treat a 3-quart casserole dish with cooking spray.
2. Put the drained sauerkraut in the bottom of the prepared dish. Add the corned beef and cheese. Spread the tomato slices in a layer over the cheese, if using.
3. Mix together the salad dressing and mayonnaise and spread over the mixture in the casserole dish.
4. Mix together the butter and rye wafers. Sprinkle the crumbs over the top of the casserole. If the wafers or bread that you used to make the crumbs don't contain caraway seeds, sprinkle some caraway seeds over the top of the crumbs.
5. Bake 30–45 minutes or until the cheese is melted and the crumb topping is browned and crunchy.

Nonstick cooking spray
1¾ cups sauerkraut, rinsed and well drained
1 pound thinly sliced corned beef
2 cups grated Swiss cheese
2 tomatoes, peeled and thinly sliced (optional)
3 tablespoons Thousand Island or Russian dressing
3 tablespoons mayonnaise
½ cup butter, melted
1 cup crumbled rye wafers
Sprinkle of caraway seeds (optional)

DRAIN YOUR SAUERKRAUT WELL
Once you've rinsed the sauerkraut and drained it in a colander, it's a good idea to dump it into a clean cotton towel. Roll up the towel around the sauerkraut and then twist the towel to wring out even more of the liquid.

Improvised Shepherd's Pie

SERVES 8-10

1. Preheat oven to 350°F.
2. Spread the meat evenly over the bottom of a 9" × 13" non-stick baking pan. Mix the onion with the oil and sprinkle the mixture over the meat. Evenly distribute the frozen vegetables over the meat and onions, then spread the gravy over the top of the vegetables.
3. In a medium bowl, mix the sour cream into the mashed potatoes; spread the potatoes over the gravy. Cover the pan with foil and bake 45 minutes.
4. Remove the foil and top with the cheese. Bake uncovered 15 minutes or until the cheese is melted.

4 cups leftover meat or cooked hamburger
1 large yellow onion, peeled and diced
1 tablespoon extra-virgin olive oil
1 (12-ounce) bag frozen peas and carrots, thawed
1 (12-ounce) bag frozen corn, thawed
1 (12-ounce) jar beef or mushroom gravy
1 cup sour cream
4 cups mashed potatoes
8 ounces Cheddar cheese, shredded

A MAKESHIFT CRUST

If you prefer a solid "crust" of sorts to the bottom of the Shepherd's Pie, mix the meat with onion, oil, 2 beaten large eggs, and a cup of crushed cornflakes or bread crumbs. This recipe is your chance to use the vegetable and gravy leftovers you've been hiding in the freezer. Thaw and bring them to room temperature before using them.

Slow-Cooked Hearty Meatballs

SERVES 8

1. Make the meatballs by mixing the ground beef with the rice, onion, garlic, parsley, dill, and egg in a large bowl; shape into small meatballs and roll each one in flour.
2. Add the tomato or tomato-vegetable juice to a 4-quart slow cooker. Carefully add the meatballs. Pour in enough water to completely cover the meatballs. Add the butter.
3. Cover and cook on low 6–8 hours, checking periodically to make sure the cooker doesn't boil dry. Add salt and pepper to taste.

1½ pounds lean ground beef
1 cup uncooked long-grain white rice
1 small yellow onion, peeled and finely chopped
3 cloves garlic, minced
2 teaspoons dried parsley
½ tablespoon dried dill
1 large egg
¼ cup all-purpose flour
2 cups tomato juice or tomato-vegetable juice
2–4 cups water
2 tablespoons butter
Salt to taste
Freshly ground black pepper to taste

Greek Meatball, Egg, and Lemon Soup

SERVES 6

1. In a large bowl, mix together the meat, minced onion, garlic, rice, parsley, dill or mint, oregano, salt, pepper, and 1 egg. Shape into small meatballs and set aside.
2. Add 2 cups of broth or water to a 4-quart slow cooker. Add the meatballs, chopped onion, carrots, potatoes, and celery, then pour in enough of the remaining broth or water to cover the meatballs and vegetables. Cook on low 6 hours.
3. In a small bowl or measuring cup, beat the 2 remaining eggs and then whisk in the corn flour. Gradually whisk in the lemon juice, and then ladle in about 1 cup of the hot broth from the slow cooker, doing so in a slow, steady stream, beating continuously until all the hot liquid has been incorporated into the egg mixture. Stir this mixture into the slow cooker, being careful not to break the meatballs. Continue to cook on low 1 hour or until thickened.

1 pound lean ground beef
¼ pound ground pork
1 small yellow onion, peeled and minced
1 clove garlic, minced
6 tablespoons uncooked long-grain white rice
1 tablespoon dried parsley
2 teaspoons dried dill or mint
1 teaspoon dried oregano
Salt to taste
Freshly ground black pepper to taste
3 large eggs
4–6 cups chicken or vegetable broth
1 medium yellow onion, peeled and chopped
1 cup baby carrots, each sliced into thirds
2 large russet potatoes, peeled and cut into cubes
1 stalk celery, finely chopped
2 tablespoons corn flour
⅓ cup fresh lemon juice

Beef-Stuffed Onions

SERVES 4-6

1. Halve the onions by cutting through the center, not from top to bottom. Scoop out the onion cores. Chop the onion cores and add to a large bowl along with the ground beef, allspice, dill, 2 tablespoons lemon juice, parsley, salt, pepper, and egg and mix well.
2. Fill the onion halves to overflowing with the meat mixture. Sprinkle the flour over the top of the meat.
3. Add the oil to a deep 3½-quart nonstick skillet or electric skillet and bring to temperature. Add the onions to the pan, meat-side down, and sauté until browned.
4. Turn the onions so that the meat side is up. Add the remaining tablespoon of lemon juice and enough water to come up to just the top of the onion. Lower the heat, cover, and simmer 1 hour or until the onion is soft and the meat is cooked through.

4 large Vidalia onions, peeled
½ pound ground beef
¼ teaspoon ground allspice
¼ teaspoon dried dill
3 tablespoons fresh lemon juice, divided
2 teaspoons dried parsley
Salt to taste
Freshly ground black pepper to taste
1 large egg
1–2 tablespoons all-purpose flour
2 tablespoons extra-virgin olive oil
Water or chicken broth

Jamaican Meat Pie Casserole

SERVES 8

1. Preheat oven to 400°F.
2. Add the ground beef, yellow and green onions, jalapeño, garlic, thyme, 1 tablespoon of the curry powder, 1 teaspoon paprika, the salt, pepper, and cayenne to a large microwave-safe bowl. Stir to combine and break the meat apart. Cover and microwave on high 3 minutes. Uncover and stir. Cover and microwave on high 3–5 minutes or until the meat is cooked through. Drain off any excess fat. Stir in the eggs, vinegar, bread crumbs, and sugar. Taste for seasoning and adjust if necessary.
3. Brush the bottom of a 14" nonstick deep-dish pizza pan or 9" × 13" nonstick baking pan with a generous amount of olive oil. Using the tips of your fingers, press 1 can of the pizza crust over the bottom of the pan. Brush the top of the crust with olive oil and sprinkle the remaining 1 tablespoon curry powder over the oil. Poke holes in the bottom crust with a fork. Top with the filling. Top the filling with the other pizza crust, carefully pressing it out to the edges of the pan.
4. Generously brush the top of the crust with extra-virgin olive oil. Sprinkle the remaining 1 teaspoon paprika over the oil. Cut several vents into the crust. Bake 30 minutes or until the crust is lightly browned on top and baked through. Let stand 10 minutes, and then cut and serve.

2 pounds lean ground beef
1 large yellow onion, peeled and diced
2 green onions, finely chopped
1 medium jalapeño pepper, seeded and minced
2 cloves garlic, minced
1 teaspoon dried thyme
2 tablespoons curry powder, divided
2 teaspoons paprika, divided
Salt to taste
Freshly ground black pepper to taste
Dash cayenne pepper
2 large eggs
1 tablespoon white or white wine vinegar
½ cup bread crumbs
½ teaspoon granulated sugar, or to taste
Extra-virgin olive oil, as needed
2 (13.8-ounce) cans refrigerated pizza crust

Armenian Meat Pie

SERVES 8

1. Preheat oven to 400°F.
2. Add the ground beef, onion, green pepper, garlic, paprika, allspice, salt, pepper, and cayenne to a large microwave-safe bowl. Stir to combine and break the meat apart. Cover and microwave on high 3 minutes. Uncover and stir. Cover and microwave on high 3–5 minutes or until meat is cooked through. Drain off any excess fat. Stir in the drained tomatoes, tomato paste, parsley, and mint.
3. Brush the bottom of a 14" nonstick deep-dish pizza pan or 9" × 13" nonstick baking pan with a generous amount of olive oil. Using the tips of your fingers, press 1 can of the pizza crust over the bottom of the pan. Poke holes in the bottom crust with a fork. Top with the filling. Top the filling with the other pizza crust, carefully pressing it out to the edges of the pan. Generously brush the top of the crust with olive oil. Cut several vents into the crust. Bake 30 minutes or until the crust is lightly browned on top and baked through. Let stand 10 minutes, then cut and serve.

2 pounds lean ground beef
1 medium yellow onion, peeled and diced
1 medium green bell pepper, seeded and diced
2 cloves garlic, minced
1 teaspoon paprika
½ teaspoon ground allspice
Salt to taste
Freshly ground black pepper to taste
Pinch cayenne pepper
1 (15-ounce) can diced tomatoes, drained
2 tablespoons tomato paste
1 tablespoon dried parsley
1 teaspoon dried mint
Extra-virgin olive oil, as needed
2 (13.8-ounce) cans refrigerated pizza crust

HAMBURGER DEEP-DISH PIZZA

To convert the Armenian Meat Pie recipe to a more traditional deep-dish pizza, substitute oregano for the mint and add 1 teaspoon of dried basil. Before you add the meat filling, cover the bottom crust with shredded mozzarella cheese to taste. You can also mix freshly grated Parmigiano-Reggiano cheese to taste into the hamburger filling.

Meatloaf with Creamy Mushroom Gravy

SERVES 8

1. Preheat oven to 350°F.
2. Put the oil, butter, garlic, onion, celery, carrot, and mushrooms in a microwave-safe bowl; cover with plastic wrap and microwave on high 30 seconds. Uncover and stir; repeat at 30-second intervals until the onions are transparent.
3. Add the red wine, bread crumbs, and milk; cover and wait 10 minutes or until the crumbs absorb the moisture in the bowl. Mix in the beef, pork, sausage, egg, parsley, paprika, salt, and pepper. Pack the mixture into a 9" × 5" loaf pan. Brush the top of the meatloaf with Worcestershire sauce if desired.
4. Cover the loaf pan with foil and bake 30 minutes. Remove the foil and bake an additional 30 minutes or until a meat thermometer inserted in the center of the meatloaf registers at least 165°F. Remove from the oven and let stand 10 minutes.
5. While the meatloaf is resting, warm the gravy in a saucepan or in the microwave. Serve with the gravy spooned over the top of the meatloaf or serve on the side in a warmed gravy boat.

1 tablespoon extra-virgin olive oil
1 teaspoon butter
3 cloves garlic, minced
1 medium yellow onion, peeled and finely chopped
2 stalks celery, finely chopped
1/2 cup peeled and grated carrots
8 ounces button or cremini mushrooms, chopped
1/4 cup dry red wine
1/2 cup fine bread crumbs
1/2 cup whole milk
3/4 pound lean ground beef
1/2 pound lean ground pork
1/4 pound mild Italian sausage
1 large egg
1 tablespoon freeze-dried parsley
1 teaspoon sweet paprika
Salt to taste
Freshly ground black pepper to taste
Worcestershire sauce (optional)
1 (10-ounce) jar beef-mushroom gravy

CRUMB WISDOM

The amount of moisture in the bowl after you microwave the vegetables can affect the amount of bread crumbs needed. If, after mixing, the mixture is too wet to form a ball, add more bread crumbs.

Unstuffed Green Peppers Casserole

SERVES 4-6

1. Preheat oven to 400°F.
2. Add the beef and onion to a 4-quart ovenproof Dutch oven; brown the hamburger over medium-high heat. Pour off any excess fat.
3. Add the tomatoes, corn, 2 cups bread crumbs, and green pepper pieces. Mix well. Cover and bake 25 minutes or until the green peppers are tender.
4. In a small bowl, mix the remaining bread crumbs with the melted butter. Remove the cover from the casserole and sprinkle the bread crumbs over the top. Bake an additional 5 minutes or until the bread crumbs are golden brown.

1 pound ground beef
1 medium yellow onion, peeled and chopped
1 (14.5-ounce) can chopped tomatoes
1 (8-ounce) can whole-kernel corn, drained
2½ cups herb-seasoned bread crumbs, divided
2 large green bell peppers, seeded and cut into large dice
1 tablespoon butter, melted

Salisbury Steak in Onion Gravy

SERVES 6-8

1. In a large bowl, mix together half of the soup with the beef, bread crumbs, egg, salt, and pepper. Shape into 6–8 patties.
2. Add the patties to a deep 3½-quart nonstick skillet or electric skillet; brown on both sides over medium-high heat, then pour off any excess fat.
3. Mix the remaining soup in a medium bowl with the remaining ingredients. Pour over the patties. Cover and simmer on low heat, stirring occasionally, 20 minutes or until the meat is cooked through and the gravy is thickened.

1 (10¾-ounce) can condensed onion soup, divided
1½ pounds lean ground beef
½ cup dry bread crumbs
1 large egg
Salt to taste
Freshly ground black pepper to taste
1 tablespoon all-purpose flour
¼ cup ketchup
¼ cup water
1 teaspoon Worcestershire sauce
½ teaspoon yellow mustard

MAKE IT AN ALL-IN-ONE DINNER

After you brown the meat patties, remove them from the pan and add a thawed 12-ounce package of frozen hash brown potatoes to the skillet. Place the meat on top of the potatoes and cook according to the directions in step 3. Add a thawed 12-ounce package of frozen baby peas, cover, and cook an additional 5 minutes or until the peas are heated through.

Meat and Vegetable "Sloppy" Sandwiches

SERVES 6

1. Add the coriander seeds to a deep 3½-quart nonstick skillet and toast 1–2 minutes over medium heat, tossing or stirring so that the seeds don't burn. Remove from the pan, cool, and coarsely chop in a coffee mill or crush under the flat side of a knife. Add the oil to the skillet and bring to temperature over medium heat; add the onions and sauté until golden. Add the garlic and sauté 1 minute. Stir in the ground beef and fry until browned, breaking it apart as it cooks.
2. Stir in the cumin, salt, and pepper. Add the carrots and sauté 1 minute. Stir in the zucchini, broth, and corn; cover and simmer 2 minutes. Uncover and simmer until most of the broth has evaporated.
3. Top with the cheese; turn off the heat and cover 1 minute or until the cheese is melted. Divide the mixture between the rolls or buns, and add ketchup and pickles if desired.

1 teaspoon coriander seeds
1 tablespoon extra-virgin olive or vegetable oil
1 medium yellow onion, peeled and chopped
2 cloves garlic, minced
1 pound ground beef
1 teaspoon ground cumin
Salt to taste
Freshly ground black pepper to taste
3 medium carrots, peeled and sliced into ¼" rounds
1 medium zucchini, halved and cut into ¼" rounds
½ cup chicken broth
1 (8-ounce) can whole-kernel corn, drained
8 ounces Cheddar cheese, grated
8 onion or Kaiser rolls
Ketchup to taste (optional)
Choice of pickles to taste (optional)

Ground Round with Cremini Mushrooms and Spinach

SERVES 4

1. Add the ground round to a nonstick skillet and cook over medium heat until no longer pink, breaking it apart while it cooks. Season with salt and pepper to taste.
2. Stir in the red pepper and the jalapeño (if using). Add the mushrooms. If additional fat is needed to sauté the mushrooms, add some butter or oil to the skillet. Sauté the mushrooms until tender.
3. Mix together the cream and egg, then stir into the meat mixture in the skillet. Bring to a boil, then lower the heat; simmer until heated through and slightly thickened.
4. To serve, put a handful of spinach on each of 4 plates. Spoon the meat and mushroom sauce over the spinach. Top each serving with Parmigiano-Reggiano to taste.

1 pound ground round
Salt to taste
Freshly ground black pepper to taste
2 tablespoons chopped roasted red pepper
1 medium jalapeño pepper, seeded and diced (optional)
8 ounces cremini mushrooms, sliced
Butter or extra-virgin olive oil, as needed (optional)
1 cup heavy cream
1 large egg, beaten
4 big handfuls baby spinach
Freshly grated Parmigiano-Reggiano cheese to taste

Marzetti Casserole

SERVES 8

1. In a 4-quart Dutch oven, prepare the egg noodles according to package directions. Drain in a colander and keep warm.
2. Brown the beef, onion, and celery in the Dutch oven over medium heat, breaking the beef apart as it cooks. Once the beef has lost its pink color and the onion is transparent, drain off any excess fat. Add the remaining ingredients except the cheeses. Lower the heat, cover, and simmer 10 minutes.
3. Stir in the noodles and Cheddar. Serve immediately, adding Parmigiano-Reggiano to the top of each serving.

8 ounces dried medium egg noodles
1 pound lean ground beef
1 medium yellow onion, peeled and chopped
2 stalks celery, diced
Salt to taste
1 (16-ounce) jar spaghetti sauce with mushrooms
1 medium green bell pepper, seeded and cut into thin strips
1 cup frozen peas
1 cup tomato juice
1 tablespoon Worcestershire sauce
$\frac{1}{2}$ teaspoon dried oregano, crushed
Freshly ground black pepper to taste
8 ounces Cheddar cheese, grated
Freshly grated Parmigiano-Reggiano cheese to taste

STEP UP THE FLAVOR

If you're baking the Marzetti Casserole the next day, you can add another flavor dimension by mixing 1 cup dried bread crumbs with 1 tablespoon melted butter or extra-virgin olive oil. Sprinkle the crumb mixture and some Parmigiano-Reggiano over the top of the casserole; bake until the casserole is heated through and the bread crumbs are golden brown.

Tamale Spoon Bread Casserole

SERVES 8-10

1. Preheat oven to 350°F.
2. Add the olive oil to a deep 3½-quart nonstick skillet and bring to temperature over medium heat; add the ground chuck and brown the meat. Add the onion, garlic, and green pepper to the skillet; cook, stirring, until the onion is slightly browned.
3. Mix together ½ cup cornmeal and 1 cup water and stir it into the skillet; cover and simmer 10 minutes.
4. Stir in the tomatoes, corn, 1 teaspoon salt, chili powder, and pepper; simmer 5 minutes longer. Mix in the olives and then spoon the meat mixture into a 3-quart casserole treated with nonstick spray.
5. Heat the milk over medium heat along with the remaining 1 teaspoon salt and the butter; once the milk begins to simmer, slowly whisk in the remaining ½ cup cornmeal. Lower the heat and continue to simmer while stirring or whisking until it thickens. Remove from the heat and stir in the cheese and eggs. Pour over the meat mixture.
6. Bake uncovered 1 hour or until the entire casserole is hot and bubbly.

1 tablespoon extra-virgin olive oil
1½ pounds ground chuck
1 large yellow onion, peeled and chopped
1 clove garlic, minced
1 medium green bell pepper, seeded and chopped
1 cup cornmeal, divided
1 cup water
2 (14.5-ounce) cans chopped tomatoes, slightly drained
1 (12-ounce) can whole-kernel corn
2 teaspoons salt, divided
1 tablespoon plus 1 teaspoon chili powder
¼ teaspoon freshly ground black pepper
½ cup sliced, pitted ripe olives
Nonstick cooking spray
1½ cups whole milk
2 tablespoons butter
1 cup grated mild Cheddar cheese
2 large eggs, slightly beaten

MAKE AHEAD

You can assemble this casserole the night before or earlier in the day. Cover the casserole dish with plastic wrap and refrigerate until needed. Remove the plastic wrap and bake 75–90 minutes. The extra cooking time lets you bake the casserole without letting it come to room temperature before you put it in the oven.

Oven-Baked Horseradish Short Ribs and Vegetables

SERVES 4

1. Preheat oven to 350°F.
2. Trim off any excess fat from of the ribs, and then arrange them in a 9" × 13" nonstick baking pan; sprinkle with salt and pepper. Bake uncovered 2 hours. Drain off any excess fat and discard.
3. Distribute the carrots, potatoes, green beans, and onions around the meat. In a measuring cup, whisk together the broth, mustard, and horseradish; pour over the meat. Tightly cover the pan with aluminum foil; bake 1½ hours or until the meat is tender. Move the meat and vegetables to a serving platter; cover and keep warm.
4. To make the sauce, strain the meat juices in the baking pan. Skim off and discard any excess fat. Add enough water to the pan juices to measure 2 cups; either return the juices to the baking pan or put in a saucepan. Bring to a boil over medium-high heat. Mix the cornstarch together with the cold water in a measuring cup or small bowl; discard any lumps. Stir the cornstarch mixture into the juices; boil 1 minute.

3 pounds beef short ribs
Salt to taste
Freshly ground black pepper to taste
1 (1-pound) bag baby carrots
4 medium russet potatoes, peeled and halved
1 (12-ounce) bag green beans, thawed
4 small white onions, halved
1 (14-ounce) can reduced-sodium beef broth
2 teaspoons mustard
2 tablespoons horseradish
2 tablespoons cornstarch
¼ cup cold water

CRUNCHY BEANS

If you prefer crisp-tender green beans, cook them separately rather than adding them to the baking pan. For this recipe, simmer them in water or broth 5–7 minutes, tasting to test for desired doneness. For extra taste, sauté 1 clove of minced garlic in oil, then add the green beans, toss to coat, and pour in the liquid.

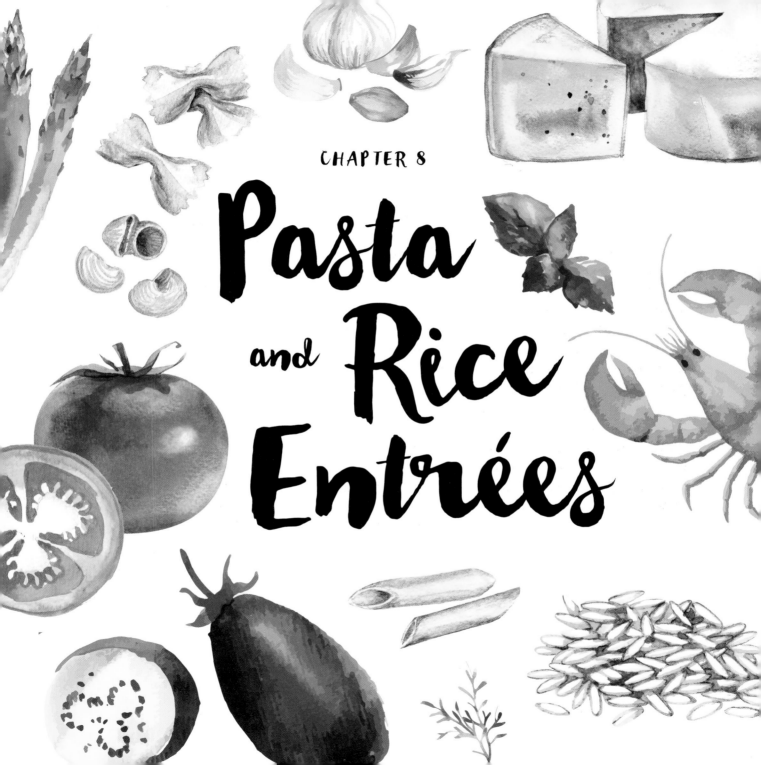

CHAPTER 8

Pasta and Rice Entrées

Shrimp and Artichoke Fettuccine

SERVES 4

1. Peel and devein the shrimp, reserving the shells. Add the shells, water, parsley, lemon slice, and pepper to a large skillet and bring to a boil over high heat; reduce heat and simmer uncovered 10 minutes. Strain and keep broth warm.
2. Cook the pasta according to the package directions; drain and set aside.
3. Add 2 tablespoons oil to the skillet and bring to temperature over medium heat; add the garlic and sauté 30 seconds. Add the artichokes and sauté 1 minute.
4. Stir in the shrimp and wine and cook until the shrimp turns pink, about 2 minutes. Stir in the tomatoes, 1 cup of the reserved shrimp broth, butter, lemon peel, salt, nutmeg, and cooked pasta; heat through.
5. To serve, place a piece of the toasted bread in each of 4 shallow soup bowls. Divide the pasta mixture among bowls, adding additional shrimp broth as desired. Garnish with the parsley and drizzle with the remaining oil. Squeeze lemon juice from 1 wedge over each serving, and garnish each with the remaining lemon wedges and grated cheese.

1 pound medium shrimp in shells
3 cups water
4 sprigs fresh parsley
1 slice lemon
1 teaspoon freshly ground black pepper
8 ounces dried fettuccine
3 tablespoons extra-virgin olive oil, divided
4 cloves garlic, minced
1 (9-ounce) package frozen artichoke hearts, thawed and halved lengthwise
½ cup dry white wine
2 plum tomatoes, finely chopped
1 tablespoon butter
1 teaspoon freshly grated lemon peel
½ teaspoon sea salt
½ teaspoon freshly ground nutmeg
4 slices Italian country loaf bread or other hearty bread, toasted
1 tablespoon finely chopped fresh Italian parsley
2 medium lemons, quartered
Freshly grated Parmigiano-Reggiano cheese to taste

Linguini in Red Clam Sauce

SERVES 4

1. In a large skillet, bring the oil to temperature over medium heat. Add the onion and sauté until transparent, about 5–7 minutes. Add the garlic and drained clams and sauté 30 seconds.
2. Stir in the clam juice, tomato paste, water, lemon juice, parsley, sugar, rosemary, and thyme. Bring to a boil, then reduce heat and simmer uncovered 15 minutes.
3. Gently stir in the cooked linguini, and cook until the pasta is brought to temperature. Serve topped with Parmigiano-Reggiano.

2 tablespoons extra-virgin olive oil
1 medium yellow onion, peeled and diced
1 clove garlic, minced
2 (6.5-ounce) cans minced clams, drained and juice reserved
1 (6-ounce) can tomato paste
1 cup water
2 tablespoons fresh lemon juice
1 tablespoon chopped fresh flat-leaf parsley
1 teaspoon granulated sugar
$\frac{1}{8}$ teaspoon dried rosemary
$\frac{1}{4}$ teaspoon dried thyme
8 ounces fresh linguini, cooked al dente
Freshly grated Parmigiano-Reggiano cheese to taste

Lobster and Fresh Mushroom Ragu

SERVES 6-8

1. In a Dutch oven or deep pot, cook the pasta in boiling water according to the package directions until al dente. Drain in a colander, set aside, and keep warm.
2. Wipe out the Dutch oven; add the oil and bring to temperature over medium heat. Add the celery and carrot; sauté 3–5 minutes or until soft. Add the onion and sauté until transparent, about 5 minutes. Add salt and pepper to taste.
3. If using tasso, add it and sauté 1 minute; if using salt pork or bacon, sauté 3 minutes or until it renders some of its fat.
4. Add all the mushrooms; stirring frequently, cook until all the mushroom liquid is rendered out. Push the mushrooms to the sides of the pan; add the tomato paste and sauté 2 minutes, then stir it into the mushrooms along with the oregano, thyme, parsley, wine, and broth, scraping the bottom of the pot to loosen any browned bits as you stir.
5. Reduce heat and simmer 20 minutes. Toss the drained pasta into the ragu sauce.
6. Remove the meat from the lobster shells; chop into large pieces. Gently stir the lobster meat into the pasta and ragu sauce. Garnish with the basil.

1½ pounds dried pappardelle or fettuccine
3 tablespoons extra-virgin olive oil
3 stalks celery, diced
3 large carrots, peeled and diced
2 medium red onions, peeled and sliced
Salt to taste
Freshly ground black pepper to taste
8 ounces tasso, salt pork, or bacon, diced
8 ounces cremini mushrooms, sliced
8 ounces portobello mushrooms, sliced
8 ounces button mushrooms, sliced
2 tablespoons tomato paste
2 teaspoons dried oregano
2 teaspoons dried thyme
1 tablespoon dried parsley
1 cup red wine
4 cups beef broth
2 (1¼-pound) cooked lobsters
¼ cup chopped fresh basil

USE THOSE LOBSTER SHELLS

You can freeze the lobster shells and use them later to make a broth to add to your favorite seafood stew or soup. Lobster broth is delicious, and it's easy to make—just simmer the shells with a roughly chopped onion, a few bay leaves, and enough water to cover everything for about 45 minutes.

Kielbasa and Roma Tomatoes Pasta

SERVES 6

1. Cook the pasta according to the package directions in a large pot. Drain; set aside and keep warm.
2. Wipe out the pot, add the oil, and bring to temperature over medium-high heat. Add the onion and sauté 1 minute. Add the kielbasa, stirring often to keep the onion from burning. Cook 5 minutes or until the onion is transparent. Add the garlic and sauté an additional 30 seconds.
3. Stir in the zucchini, bell pepper, Italian seasoning, and cayenne pepper; cook and stir 5 minutes.
4. Stir in the tomatoes and cooked pasta. Cook until heated through, stirring occasionally. Add salt and pepper to taste.

2 cups dried rotini or rotelle pasta (about 6 ounces)
1 tablespoon olive oil
1 medium yellow onion, peeled and cut into wedges
1 pound cooked kielbasa, halved lengthwise and sliced diagonally
2 cloves garlic, minced
1 small zucchini, cut into matchstick-sized strips
1 medium yellow or orange bell pepper, seeded and diced
1 teaspoon dried Italian seasoning, crushed
Pinch cayenne pepper
8 Roma tomatoes (about 1 pound), cored and chopped
Salt to taste
Freshly ground black pepper to taste

Shrimp and Radicchio Fettuccine

SERVES 4

1. In a large Dutch oven cook the fettuccine according to package directions. Drain, set aside, and keep warm.
2. Wipe out the pan, add the oil, and bring to temperature over medium heat. Add the squash, onion, and garlic; sauté 3 minutes or until the onion and squash begin to soften.
3. Add the shrimp; sauté 3 minutes or until the shrimp are opaque. Reduce heat and stir in the broth, cream, and hot sauce (if using).
4. Remove from heat; whisk in the cream cheese, stirring until the cheese is melted into the sauce. Stir in the cooked fettuccine, basil, lemon peel, mint, salt, and pepper.
5. Add the radicchio and cherry tomatoes; stir until the radicchio is wilted. Serve topped with Parmigiano-Reggiano.

8 ounces garlic-basil or tomato-basil dried fettuccine
1 tablespoon extra-virgin olive oil
6 ounces baby pattypan squash, halved or quartered
1 small red onion, peeled and diced
1 clove garlic, minced
8 ounces small shrimp, peeled and deveined
½ cup chicken broth
½ cup heavy cream
½ teaspoon hot sauce (optional)
4 ounces cream cheese, cut into small pieces
3 tablespoons chopped fresh basil
2 teaspoons grated lemon peel
1 teaspoon chopped fresh mint
Salt to taste
Freshly ground black pepper to taste
1 small head radicchio, torn
1 cup halved cherry tomatoes
Freshly grated Parmigiano-Reggiano cheese to taste

HERB HELP
Fresh herbs, especially basil, are the most tasty and aromatic when they're raw or only exposed to heat for a short time. On the other hand, dried herbs take some time to draw out the flavor. Therefore, if you're using dried herbs in this recipe, consider adding them when you sauté the shrimp.

Mexican-Style Baked Pasta

SERVES 6

1. Preheat oven to 375°F.
2. In a large Dutch oven or oven-safe pan melt the butter over medium heat. Add the onion and bell pepper and sauté 5 minutes. Stir in the flour, salt, cilantro, and cumin. Whisk in the milk and cook until thickened and bubbly, about 8–10 minutes.
3. Reduce heat to low; add the Colby and half of the Monterey jack. Stir until the cheese is melted.
4. Add the cooked pasta, salsa, and olives to the pan; stir to combine. Sprinkle with the remaining Monterey jack. Sprinkle lightly with chili powder.
5. Bake uncovered 20 minutes or until bubbly around edges and heated through. Let stand 5 minutes before serving.

12 ounces bow tie pasta, cooked
3 tablespoons butter
1 medium yellow onion, peeled and diced
1 medium red bell pepper, seeded and chopped
⅓ cup all-purpose flour
½ teaspoon salt
1 teaspoon dried cilantro, crushed
½ teaspoon ground cumin
3 cups whole milk
6 ounces Colby cheese, cubed
6 ounces Monterey jack cheese, grated, divided
1 cup bottled salsa
⅔ cup halved pitted green and/or ripe olives
Chili powder to taste

Skillet Ravioli

SERVES 4

1. Add the pasta sauce, sugar, and water to a 10" skillet. Bring to boil over medium-high heat. Add salt and pepper to taste.
2. Stir in the ravioli. Reduce heat and cover; cook, stirring occasionally, about 5 minutes or until the ravioli are tender.
3. Add the egg, ricotta, and grated cheese to a bowl and stir to combine.
4. Top the ravioli with the spinach and then spoon the cheese mixture on top of the spinach. Cover and cook over low heat about 10 minutes or until the cheese layer is set.

2 cups pasta sauce of your choice
¼ teaspoon granulated sugar
⅓ cup water
Salt to taste
Freshly ground black pepper to taste
1 (9-ounce) package frozen ravioli
1 large egg, lightly beaten
1 (15-ounce) carton ricotta cheese
¼ cup grated Romano or Parmigiano-Reggiano cheese, or more to taste
1 (10-ounce) package frozen chopped spinach, thawed and drained

Slow-Cooked Chicken, Mushroom, and Tortellini

SERVES 4-6

1. Add the mushrooms, undrained tomatoes, red pepper, onion, wine or broth, tapioca, vinegar, and garlic to a 4- or 6-quart slow cooker. Stir to combine.
2. Place the chicken on top of the sauce. Sprinkle the salt, paprika, and pepper over the chicken. Cover and cook on low 8–9 hours.
3. Remove the chicken and keep warm. Add the tortellini to the sauce; cover and cook on high 10–15 minutes or until the pasta is done.
4. Arrange the chicken on a serving platter and top with the pasta and sauce. Top with grated cheese, if desired.

2 cups sliced button or cremini mushrooms

1 (14.5-ounce) can diced tomatoes with Italian herbs

1 medium red bell pepper, seeded and diced

1 medium yellow onion, peeled and thinly sliced

¼ cup dry red wine or beef broth

2 tablespoons quick-cooking tapioca

2 tablespoons balsamic vinegar

3 cloves garlic, minced

2½ pounds bone-in chicken breasts, skin removed

¼ teaspoon salt

¼ teaspoon paprika

¼ teaspoon freshly ground black pepper

1 (9-ounce) package fresh or frozen cheese tortellini

Freshly grated Parmigiano-Reggiano cheese to taste

Seafood Pasta

SERVES 4-6

1. In a large Dutch oven or stockpot, cook the pasta to al dente according to package directions. Drain, set aside, and keep warm.
2. Wipe out the pan. Add the oil and bring to temperature over medium heat. Add the celery; sauté 3–5 minutes or until soft. Add the onion and sauté until transparent, about 5 minutes. Add the garlic and sauté an additional 30 seconds.
3. Stir in the dried herbs, salt, black pepper, red pepper, and tomatoes. Add the wine or broth; bring to a simmer and then add the butter, fish, and clams or mussels. Cover and simmer about 5 minutes.
4. Add the shrimp; simmer until the shrimp are firm and pink in color. Serve over the pasta, topped with parsley.

1 pound dried linguini
2 tablespoons extra-virgin olive oil
2 stalks celery, diced
1 small yellow onion, peeled and diced
4 cloves garlic, minced
½ teaspoon dried basil
¼ teaspoon dried dill
¼ teaspoon dried fennel
Salt to taste
½ teaspoon freshly ground black pepper
Pinch dried red pepper flakes
1 (16-ounce) can diced tomatoes
½ cup white wine or chicken broth
¼ cup butter
1 pound grouper, salmon, or snapper, cut into bite-sized pieces
1 (10-ounce) can boiled baby clams or 6.5-ounce can whole shelled mussels
½ pound medium shrimp, peeled and deveined
¼ cup chopped fresh flat-leaf parsley

Simplified Baked Lasagna

SERVES 8-10

1. Add the beef, onion, oregano, garlic, salt, and pepper to a large Dutch oven; brown the meat over medium heat, stirring it with the other ingredients in the pan and breaking it apart as it cooks. When the meat is cooked through, drain off any excess fat.
2. Stir in the pasta sauce and sugar. Pour the water in the emptied pasta sauce jar; cover and shake to rinse out the jar. Add the water to the pan and stir into the meat mixture. Remove the pan from the heat; stir in half of the grated mozzarella and the cottage cheese. Pour sauce into a bowl.
3. Preheat oven to 350°F.
4. Wipe out the Dutch oven and spray lightly with nonstick cooking spray. To assemble the lasagna, ladle in enough of the sauce to cover the bottom pan. Sprinkle Parmigiano-Reggiano over the top of the sauce if desired. Break the pasta noodles in half and create a layer of the noodles on the bottom of the pot. Repeat layering until all the noodles are in the pan and covered. Sprinkle the remaining grated mozzarella cheese over the top, along with some additional Parmigiano-Reggiano if desired.
5. Cover with foil and bake 50 minutes. Remove the foil and bake an additional 15 minutes or until the cheese on top is melted, bubbling, and lightly browned. Remove from the oven and let sit 10 minutes before serving.

1 pound lean ground beef
1 tablespoon dried minced onion
1 teaspoon dried oregano, crushed
1 teaspoon dried minced garlic
Salt to taste
Freshly ground black pepper to taste
1 (45-ounce) jar pasta sauce
½ teaspoon granulated sugar
½ cup water
1 pound mozzarella cheese, grated, divided
1 (16-ounce) container cottage cheese
Nonstick cooking spray
Freshly grated Parmigiano-Reggiano cheese to taste (optional)
1 pound dried lasagna noodles

SAUSAGE LASAGNA

If you prefer to skip the "browning the hamburger" step, you can instead substitute a pound of diced cooked smoked sausage. Use all the other ingredients; however, because you will not be heating the pasta sauce before you assemble the lasagna, bake the lasagna covered 1 hour and then uncovered 15 minutes.

Florentine Lasagna

SERVES 8

1. Squeeze the moisture out of the thawed spinach, and then thoroughly dry it in a salad spinner or between cotton towels.

2. Add the ground beef, onion, and garlic to a deep 3½-quart nonstick skillet or large saucepan over medium heat. Stir-fry until the meat is browned and the onion is transparent, about 8 minutes. Drain off and discard any excess fat.

3. Stir in the tomato juice, mushrooms, tomato paste, Worcestershire, oregano, parsley, salt, and pepper. Bring to a simmer, lower the heat, and simmer uncovered 30 minutes, stirring occasionally.

4. Preheat oven to 350°F.

5. To prepare the lasagna, treat a 9" × 13" nonstick baking pan with nonstick spray; layer half of the noodles, half of the hot prepared sauce, half of the ricotta, half of the Parmigiano-Reggiano, half of the Romano, half of the mozzarella cheese, and all the spinach. Then repeat another layer in that order. Cover with aluminum foil and let rest 30 minutes.

6. Leave the aluminum foil cover in place and bake 50 minutes. Remove the foil and continue baking 20 minutes. Remove from the oven, cover, and let stand 20 minutes before cutting.

2 (10-ounce) packages frozen spinach, thawed
1 pound lean ground chuck
1 large yellow onion, peeled and diced
3 cloves garlic, minced
4 cups tomato juice
8 ounces button mushrooms, sliced
1 (6-ounce) can tomato paste
1 tablespoon Worcestershire sauce
1 teaspoon dried oregano, crushed
1 teaspoon dried parsley, crushed
½ teaspoon salt
½ teaspoon freshly ground black pepper
Nonstick cooking spray
8 ounces dried lasagna noodles, uncooked
15 ounces ricotta cheese
1½ cups freshly grated Parmigiano-Reggiano cheese, divided
1½ cups freshly grated Romano cheese, divided
2 cups grated mozzarella cheese, divided

BAKING A BETTER LASAGNA

This recipe tastes best if you make the sauce in advance and refrigerate it for a day or two so the flavors can blend; the added bonus is that then when you're ready to prepare the lasagna, technically you'll only be using that one pot (well, baking pan) to make your meal.

Polynesian Turkey and Noodles

SERVES 4–6

1. In a Dutch oven, cook the egg noodles according to the package directions. Drain in a colander; set aside and keep warm.
2. Add the egg to a small bowl and beat lightly. Put ¼ cup cornstarch in another bowl. Dip each chunk of turkey in the egg, and then roll it in the cornstarch.
3. Add the oil to the Dutch oven and bring it to temperature over medium heat; brown the turkey pieces in the oil. Remove them with a slotted spoon and let them rest atop the egg noodles in the colander.
4. Add enough water to the reserved pineapple juice to make 1 cup; carefully add it to the oil in the Dutch oven along with the sugar, vinegar, and green pepper. Bring to a boil, stirring constantly. Reduce heat and simmer 2 minutes.
5. Blend 2 tablespoons cornstarch with the cold water and add it to the pineapple juice mixture. Heat, stirring constantly, until it thickens and boils; boil 1 additional minute.
6. Stir in the pineapple chunks, soy sauce, carrots, and cooked turkey. Cook until all the ingredients are heated through.
7. To serve, either divide the noodles between serving plates and spoon the turkey-pineapple mixture over the noodles or add the noodles to the turkey-pineapple mixture and gently stir to combine.

1 (8-ounce) package dried egg noodles
1 large egg
¼ cup plus 2 tablespoons cornstarch
2 cups cubed turkey
2 tablespoons peanut or vegetable oil
1 (13.5-ounce) can pineapple chunks, drained (reserve juice)
½ cup granulated sugar
½ cup apple cider vinegar
1 medium green bell pepper, seeded and cut into strips
¼ cup cold water
1 teaspoon soy sauce
4 large carrots, peeled, cooked, and cut into 1" pieces

Jambalaya

SERVES 6-8

1. Add the bacon fat or oil to a large Dutch oven or stockpot and bring it to temperature over medium heat. Shred 8 of the baby carrots. Add the shredded carrots, celery, and green peppers to the pan; sauté 3–5 minutes or until soft.
2. Add the yellow and green onions and sauté until transparent, about 5 minutes. Add the garlic and sauté an additional 30 seconds.
3. Stir in the smoked sausage and stir-fry 3 minutes; add the ham and stir-fry 1 minute. Chop the remaining carrots and add them to the pan.
4. Stir in the tomatoes, pork or chicken, broth, parsley, thyme, hot sauce, and Worcestershire. Bring to a boil, and then stir in the rice; reduce heat, cover, and simmer 20 minutes.
5. Fluff the rice; add additional water if needed. If the shrimp are large, cut them in half; otherwise, add the shrimp to the pot, cover, and cook another 3–5 minutes or until the shrimp are cooked. If excess moisture remains in the dish, uncover and cook until it's evaporated, stirring often to keep the rice from sticking. Add salt and pepper to taste.

3 tablespoons bacon fat or peanut oil

1 (1-pound) bag baby carrots, divided

4 stalks celery, diced

2 medium green bell peppers, seeded and chopped

1 large yellow onion, peeled and diced

6 green onions, chopped

3 cloves garlic, minced

½ pound smoked sausage, thinly sliced

½ pound cooked ham, diced

2 (15-ounce) cans diced tomatoes, drained

1 (28-ounce) can heat-and-serve pork or chicken, undrained

3 cups chicken broth

1 tablespoon dried parsley

1 teaspoon dried thyme

½ teaspoon hot sauce, or to taste

¼ cup Worcestershire sauce

2 cups uncooked long-grain rice

Water, as needed

1 pound medium or large shrimp, peeled and deveined

Salt to taste

Freshly ground black pepper to taste

Shrimp Étouffée

SERVES 6

1. Add the bacon fat or oil and flour to a large Dutch oven or stockpot over medium heat. Cook about 15 minutes or until the roux is the color of peanut butter, stirring constantly so it doesn't burn.
2. Stir in the green pepper, celery, carrot (if using), and yellow and green onions. Sauté 10 minutes or until the vegetables are tender. Add the garlic, tomato sauce, broth, and wine, stirring constantly until the mixture thickens.
3. Add the bay leaves, basil, thyme, and hot sauce; stir to combine. Cover, reduce heat, and simmer 45 minutes.
4. Add the shrimp and simmer 20 minutes, uncovered. Remove and discard the bay leaves. Add salt and pepper to taste. Serve over cooked rice, garnished with parsley if desired.

3 tablespoons bacon fat or peanut oil
3 tablespoons all-purpose flour
1 small green bell pepper, seeded and chopped
3 stalks celery, diced
1 large carrot, peeled and shredded (optional)
1 large yellow onion, peeled and diced
4 green onions, chopped
3 cloves garlic, minced
3 tablespoons tomato sauce
1¼ cups beef broth
1 cup dry white wine
2 bay leaves
¼ teaspoon dried basil
¼ teaspoon dried thyme
1 teaspoon hot sauce, or to taste
1½ pounds medium shrimp, peeled and deveined
Salt to taste
Freshly ground black pepper to taste
3 cups cooked rice
¼ cup chopped fresh flat-leaf parsley (optional)

Red Beans and Rice

SERVES 6-8

1. Add all the ingredients except the cooked rice to a 4-quart Dutch oven or stockpot. Add additional water if needed to bring the liquid level to just above the other ingredients in the pot.
2. Cover and simmer 1 hour, stirring occasionally and checking to make sure the pan doesn't boil dry. Serve over the cooked rice.

MAKE YOUR OWN PICKLED PORK

Add ¼ cup mustard seed, ½ tablespoon celery seed, 1 tablespoon hot sauce, 2 cups white vinegar, ½ bay leaf, ½ tablespoon kosher salt, 6 peppercorns, and 3 smashed cloves of garlic to a nonreactive pan; boil for 3 minutes. Allow to cool, then pour over 1 pound of cooked cubed pork and cover. Pickled pork will keep in the refrigerator for up to 3 days.

3 (15-ounce) cans kidney beans, rinsed and drained

2 cups water or chicken broth, or more as needed

1 medium yellow onion, peeled and diced

1 bunch green onions, chopped

7 cloves garlic, minced

2 tablespoons dried parsley

1 stalk celery, diced

½ cup ketchup

1 medium green bell pepper, seeded and diced

1 tablespoon Worcestershire sauce

2 teaspoons hot sauce, or to taste

2 bay leaves

¼ teaspoon dried thyme

1 pound smoked sausage, sliced

1 pound pickled pork, cut into cubes

Salt to taste

Freshly ground black pepper to taste

3–4 cups cooked rice

Paella

SERVES 6-8

1. Bring the oil to temperature over medium-high heat in a 15" paella pan or deep skillet. Stir in the bell pepper and onions; sauté 5 minutes or until the onions are transparent.
2. Add the garlic, chicken, and pork; stir-fry until the meat is lightly browned. Stir in the ham, chorizo, and rice; sauté until the rice begins to color.
3. Add the chicken broth and bring to a boil. Stir in the saffron, annatto oil, paprika, and salt. Reduce heat to medium and cover; cook 10 minutes, rotating the pan or stirring the contents of the pan occasionally. Check the rice; cover and cook until the rice is tender, about 5–10 more minutes.
4. Stir in the peas, shrimp, mussels, clams, and wine. Cover and cook 5 minutes or until the shrimp is opaque and the mussels and clams are warm. Garnish with lemon slices and serve.

ARBORIO RICE

Arborio rice is an Italian medium-grain rice. It has a high starch content, which creates a creamy base. This is why the firmer rounded grains are often used in paella and risotto dishes in Mediterranean cuisine.

½ cup extra-virgin olive oil
1 medium red bell pepper, seeded and diced
2 medium yellow onions, peeled and diced
2 cloves garlic, minced
1 pound boneless chicken thighs, skin removed and diced
½ pound ground pork
1 cup diced smoked ham
1 cup sliced chorizo
2 cups uncooked Arborio or converted rice
3 cups chicken broth
⅛ teaspoon saffron threads, crushed
2 tablespoons annatto oil
1 teaspoon paprika
Salt to taste
1 cup frozen peas, thawed
½ pound medium shrimp, peeled and deveined
1 (6.5-ounce) can mussels, rinsed and drained
1 (10-ounce) can boiled baby clams, rinsed and drained
1 cup dry white wine
1 medium lemon, thinly sliced

Gumbo

SERVES 6-8

1. Add the lard or oil and flour to a large Dutch oven or stock-pot over medium heat. Cook 15 minutes or until the roux is the color of peanut butter, stirring constantly so it doesn't burn.
2. Stir in the celery, onions, green pepper, garlic, and tomatoes; cook, stirring constantly, until the vegetables are tender. Add the remaining ingredients except the sausage, chicken, salt, pepper, and rice and simmer covered over medium heat 30–45 minutes or until the mixture thickens.
3. Stir in the sausage and chicken; simmer uncovered an additional 15 minutes. Add salt and pepper to taste.
4. Serve hot over about 1/4 cup of rice per serving.

1/4 cup lard or peanut oil
1/4 cup all-purpose flour
4 stalks celery, chopped
1 large yellow onion, peeled and diced
1 medium green bell pepper, seeded and diced
3 cloves garlic, minced
1 (15-ounce) can diced tomatoes
1/4 teaspoon dried thyme
1/4 teaspoon dried basil
3 bay leaves
2 tablespoons filé powder
2 tablespoons Worcestershire sauce
1 teaspoon hot sauce, or to taste
8 cups chicken broth
1 pound smoked sausage, sliced
2 cups shredded cooked chicken
Salt to taste
Freshly ground black pepper to taste
4 1/2 cups cooked long-grain rice

Dirty Rice

SERVES 4

1. Add the bacon fat or oil to a large Dutch oven or stockpot and bring to temperature over medium heat. Add the green pepper and celery; sauté 3 minutes. Add the yellow onion; sauté 5 minutes or until the onions are transparent and the vegetables are tender. Add the garlic and sauté 30 seconds.
2. Stir in the ground pork and sausage; fry until the meat is lightly browned. Drain off and discard any excess fat.
3. Stir in the chicken broth and bring to a boil. Add the chicken livers, cover, and lightly boil 30 minutes. Use a slotted spoon to remove the chicken livers; set them aside to cool.
4. Stir in the Worcestershire, cayenne, parsley, and rice; bring to a boil. Reduce heat to medium-low, cover, and cook 15 minutes.
5. Chop the chicken livers. Stir into the rice mixture. Cover and simmer 20 minutes; stir occasionally to keep the rice from sticking. Add water if additional moisture is needed. Stir in the green onion. Add salt and pepper to taste.

2 tablespoons bacon fat or peanut oil
1 small green bell pepper, seeded and diced
2 stalks celery, chopped
1 medium yellow onion, peeled and diced
1 clove garlic, minced
½ pound lean ground pork
½ pound Italian sausage
3 cups chicken broth
1 pound chicken livers
½ tablespoon Worcestershire sauce
Cayenne pepper to taste
1 tablespoon dried parsley
1 cup uncooked long-grain rice
Water, as needed
2 green onions, chopped
Salt to taste
Freshly ground black pepper to taste

Spanish Rice

SERVES 4

1. Add the meat, onion, green pepper, and chili powder to a deep 2-quart or larger nonstick skillet; fry the hamburger over medium to medium-high heat, stirring frequently to prevent the vegetables from burning and to break apart the meat. When the meat is browned and the onions are transparent, drain off and discard any excess fat.
2. Stir in the water, sugar, tomato sauce, butter, rice, Worcestershire, hot sauce, and thyme; bring to a boil. Reduce heat to low, cover, and simmer 25 minutes or until the rice is tender. Add salt and pepper to taste.

1 pound ground beef
1 medium yellow onion, peeled and diced
1 medium green bell pepper, seeded and diced
1 teaspoon chili powder
1½ cups water
Pinch light brown or granulated sugar
½ cup tomato sauce
1 tablespoon butter
1 cup uncooked short- or medium-grain rice
2 tablespoons Worcestershire sauce
Hot sauce to taste
¼ teaspoon dried thyme
Salt to taste
Freshly ground black pepper to taste

Stuffed Peppers

SERVES 8

1. Preheat oven to 350°F.
2. Cut the tops off of the green peppers. Remove the seeds from the peppers and discard. Set the peppers in a 9" × 13" non-stick baking pan and set the tops aside.
3. Add the beef, rice, eggs, garlic, onion, butter, salt, black pepper, and allspice or nutmeg (if using) to a large bowl; mix well. Divide the meat filling mixture between the green peppers; place the tops on each.
4. In the bowl, mix together the tomato sauce, wine or vinegar, sugar, and broth. Pour into the pan holding the stuffed green peppers.
5. Treat one side of a large piece of heavy-duty aluminum foil with nonstick cooking spray. Tent the foil over the baking pan, treated-side down; crimp the edges to form a seal.
6. Bake 45 minutes. Remove the foil, being careful to avoid being burned by the escaping steam. Return to the oven and bake an additional 15 minutes or until the peppers are tender and the filling is cooked through. Sprinkle each pepper with a generous topping of Parmesan cheese and serve.

8 medium green bell peppers
2 pounds lean ground beef
2 cups cooked rice
3 large eggs
3 cloves garlic, minced
1 large yellow onion, peeled and diced
¼ cup butter
Salt to taste
Freshly ground black pepper to taste
Pinch allspice or nutmeg (optional)
1 cup tomato sauce
2 tablespoons white wine or white wine vinegar
1 tablespoon granulated sugar
1 cup chicken broth
Nonstick cooking spray
⅓ cup grated Parmesan cheese

STUFFED PEPPER OPTIONS

While rice is traditional in this dish, you can substitute a cup of bread crumbs or cracker crumbs for the cooked rice. Or, replace some of the rice in the meat mixture with peeled and chopped hard-boiled eggs. Or, use a mixture of ground beef and ground pork or lamb.

Sweet-and-Sour Pork

SERVES 4

1. Bring the oil to temperature over medium-high heat in a nonstick wok or large skillet. Add the pork and garlic powder; stir-fry 5 minutes or until the pork is browned.
2. Drain the pineapple, reserving the juice. Set aside the pineapple tidbits. Add water to the pineapple juice to bring the total amount of liquid to 2½ cups. Add to the wok or skillet along with the vinegar, soy sauce, and sugar (if using). Bring to a boil; reduce heat to low, cover, and simmer 20 minutes.
3. Remove the cover and stir in the rice. Cover and simmer another 25 minutes or until all the liquid is absorbed and the pork is tender.
4. Stir in the green pepper, tomato, pineapple tidbits, and stir-fry vegetables mix. Cover and cook on low 5 minutes. Uncover and stir-fry until the vegetables are cooked to crisp-tender. Serve immediately.

1 tablespoon peanut oil

1 pound lean pork, cut into bite-sized pieces

1 teaspoon garlic powder

1 (13.5-ounce) can pineapple tidbits

Water, as needed

¼ cup white vinegar

1 teaspoon soy sauce

2 tablespoons granulated sugar (optional)

1 cup uncooked converted white rice

1 medium green bell pepper, seeded and diced

1 medium tomato, diced

1 (16-ounce) bag frozen stir-fry vegetables mix, thawed

Southwestern Chicken and Rice Casserole

SERVES 6

1. Preheat oven to 425°F.
2. Bring the oil to temperature over medium heat in a large ovenproof Dutch oven; add the onion and sauté 5 minutes or until transparent. Stir in the rice and vermicelli mix (including the seasoning packet); cook and stir 2 minutes.
3. Stir in the broth and water; bring to a boil. Reduce heat, cover, and simmer 20 minutes.
4. Stir in the chicken, tomatoes, chilies, basil, chili powder, cumin, and pepper. Cover and bake 25 minutes. Sprinkle with the cheese. Let stand 5 minutes before serving.

1 tablespoon extra-virgin olive oil
1 medium yellow onion, peeled and diced
1 (6.9-ounce) package chicken-flavored rice and vermicelli mix
1 (14-ounce) can chicken broth
2 cups water
2 cups chopped cooked chicken or turkey
1 (15-ounce) can diced tomatoes
3 tablespoons canned green chilies, drained and diced
1 teaspoon dried basil, crushed
1½ teaspoons chili powder
⅛ teaspoon ground cumin
⅛ teaspoon freshly ground black pepper
2 ounces Cheddar cheese, shredded

Chicken, Broccoli, and Rice Casserole

SERVES 8

1. Preheat oven to 400°F.
2. Add the butter and oil to a large ovenproof Dutch oven and bring it to temperature over medium-high heat; swirl the pan to blend the butter and oil. Add the mushrooms; cook and stir 2 minutes.
3. Add the onion and chicken; stir-fry until the chicken is just cooked through. Stir in the garlic and stir-fry another 30 seconds.
4. Add the undiluted mushroom soup and the cheese spread or Velveeta. Stir until the cheese is melted.
5. Remove the Dutch oven from the heat. Stir in the rice, broccoli, water chestnuts, sour cream, and pepper. Bake uncovered 15–20 minutes.
6. Remove from the oven and top with the Cheddar and bread crumbs or crushed croutons. Return to oven and bake 10 minutes or until the cheese is melted and the topping is lightly browned.

1 tablespoon butter
1 teaspoon vegetable oil
1 cup chopped button mushrooms
1 small yellow onion, peeled and diced
1 pound boneless, skinless chicken breasts, cut into bite-sized pieces
2 cloves garlic, minced
1 (10¾-ounce) can condensed cream of mushroom soup
1 cup cubed pasteurized processed cheese spread or Velveeta
1 (14-ounce) box Uncle Ben's Whole-Grain Brown or Original Long-Grain Instant Rice
1 (12-ounce) bag frozen broccoli florets, thawed and drained
1 (8-ounce) can sliced water chestnuts, drained
½ cup sour cream
¼ teaspoon freshly ground black pepper
4 ounces Cheddar cheese, shredded
½ cup bread crumbs or crushed croutons

Shrimp and Rice Casserole

SERVES 6

1. Preheat oven to 325°F.
2. Add the water to a large ovenproof Dutch oven and bring to a boil over medium-high heat. Add the salt and shrimp; boil 1 minute. Drain immediately and set the shrimp aside.
3. Wipe out the Dutch oven and melt the butter in it; add the green pepper and onion, and sauté 5 minutes or until the onion is transparent.
4. Stir in the shrimp, rice, soup, 1½ cups cheese, and peas. Add salt and pepper to taste. Top with the remaining ½ cup cheese.
5. Bake uncovered 30 minutes or until the cheese is melted and bubbly.

2 cups water
½ tablespoon salt
1 pound medium shrimp, peeled and deveined
2 tablespoons butter
½ medium green bell pepper, seeded and chopped
1 small Vidalia onion, peeled and diced
3 cups cooked rice
1 (10¾-ounce) can condensed cream of mushroom soup
8 ounces sharp Cheddar cheese, grated
1 cup frozen baby peas, thawed
Salt to taste
Freshly ground black pepper to taste

Puerto Rican Rice and Pigeon Peas

SERVES 8

1. Add the gandules and water to a 6-quart Dutch oven; bring to a boil over medium heat. Cover and turn off the heat; allow to sit 1 hour. Drain, reserving 1½ cups of the water.
2. Add the oil, salt pork or bacon, and ham to the Dutch oven and sauté over medium heat 3 minutes. Add the garlic, bell peppers, and onion; sauté until the onion is transparent, about 5 minutes.
3. Add the tomato, drained gandules, and reserved water. Bring to a boil; cover, lower the heat, and simmer 15 minutes or until the gandules are almost tender and have absorbed most of the liquid.
4. Stir in the annatto oil and broth or water. Bring to a boil over medium heat. Add the rice, cover, and turn off the burner; let sit 30 minutes or until the liquid is absorbed and the rice is tender. Stir to fluff the rice. Add salt and pepper to taste.

½ pound dried gandules (pigeon peas)
3 cups water
1 tablespoon extra-virgin olive oil
1 ounce salt pork or bacon, chopped
2 ounces cooked ham, chopped
2 cloves garlic, minced
1 medium red bell pepper, seeded and diced
1 medium green bell pepper, seeded and diced
1 large yellow onion, peeled and diced
1 medium tomato, finely chopped
1 tablespoon annatto oil
2 cups chicken broth or water
1 cup instant white rice
Salt to taste
Freshly ground black pepper to taste

Microwave Chicken and Rice

SERVES 2

1. Heat the rice pouch in the microwave according to package directions.
2. Remove the skin and breast meat from the chicken; discard the skin and reserve the breast meat for another use. Shred the remaining meat.
3. Add the chicken to a covered microwave-safe bowl large enough to hold all the ingredients; microwave at 70 percent power for 1 minute. Stir. Repeat until the chicken is brought to temperature.
4. Toss the broth or water, onions, rice, peas, stir-fry sauce, oil, and soy sauce and honey (if using) with the chicken and microwave 1 minute at 70 percent power. If the mixture is not sufficiently heated, repeat 1 more minute. Top with the almonds.

1 (8.8-ounce) microwaveable pouch brown rice
1 (3-pound) rotisserie chicken
1 tablespoon chicken broth or water
2 green onions, sliced
1/2 cup frozen peas
1/4 cup bottled stir-fry sauce
1/4 teaspoon toasted sesame oil
Soy sauce to taste (optional)
Honey to taste (optional)
1/4 cup sliced almonds

Lobster Paella

SERVES 6

1. Preheat oven to 425°F.
2. Add the oil to a large Dutch oven and bring it to temperature over medium heat. Add the onions and sauté 5 minutes, stirring occasionally. Add the bell peppers; sauté 5 minutes.
3. Lower the heat; add the garlic and sauté 1 minute. Stir in the rice, broth, saffron, red pepper flakes, salt, and pepper; bring to a boil over medium-high heat.
4. Cover, move the pot to the oven, and bake 15 minutes. Take the pot out of the oven and remove the lid; gently stir the rice using a wooden spoon. Return the pot to the oven and bake uncovered 10–15 minutes or until the rice is fully cooked.
5. Move the paella back to the stovetop; add the liqueur. Cook over medium heat 1 minute or until the liqueur is absorbed by the rice. Turn off the heat and add the lobster, kielbasa, and peas, gently stirring to mix.
6. Cover and let sit 10 minutes. Uncover, sprinkle with the parsley, garnish with lemon wedges, and serve hot.

¼ cup extra-virgin olive oil
2 large yellow onions, peeled and diced
2 medium red bell peppers, seeded and sliced into ½" strips
4 cloves garlic, minced
2 cups uncooked white basmati rice
5 cups chicken broth
½ teaspoon saffron threads, crushed
¼ teaspoon crushed red pepper flakes
1 teaspoon sea or kosher salt
½ teaspoon freshly ground black pepper
⅓ cup licorice-flavored liqueur, such as Pernod
1½ pounds cooked lobster meat
1 pound kielbasa, cut into ¼" rounds
1 (10-ounce) package frozen peas
Chopped fresh flat-leaf parsley to taste
2 medium lemons, cut into wedges

Appendix A: Equipment

Your cooking equipment can make a difference in the ease with which you can prepare foods. Buy the best you can afford. Better pan construction equals more even heat distribution, which translates to reduced cooking time and more even cooking. Better doesn't always have to be the newest and most expensive pan on the market. A well-seasoned cast-iron skillet can go from the stovetop to the oven. Other considerations, like glass lids for saucepans and skillets, can cut the cooking time because they let you see the food cooking inside the pot. You don't have to remove the lid as much, so less heat escapes.

MR. BAR-B-Q
This company produces over 400 products including the Beer Can Chicken Roaster, a nonstick "beer can chicken" pan insert that holds the seasoning liquid and onto which you mount the chicken during the baking process; it can also be set directly on an outdoor grill.
www.mrbarbq.com

CHICAGO METALLIC
This company sells Chicago Metallic custom baking pans and other products.
www.cmbakeware.com

CUISINART
Probably best known for their innovative food processors, Cuisinart also has a wide selection of countertop appliances and cookware, including toaster ovens, rotisseries, fondue pots, microwave ovens, pressure cookers, food processors, and slow cookers.
www.cuisinart.com

HEARTH KITCHEN
Hearth Kitchen's HearthKit Ceramic Oven Insert is a three-piece insert that fits into your oven and turns your oven into a hearth oven. You can make artesian breads, roast chicken and turkey, brick-oven pizzas, and more.
www.hearth-oven.com

LE CREUSET
This company sells high-quality enameled cast-iron Dutch ovens, roasters, soup pots, and other pans.
www.lecreuset.com

KAISER BAKEWARE
This company sells springform pans and other quality bakeware.
www.wmfamericas.com/shop/

PLEASANT HILL GRAIN
A full-service distributor for a wide variety of helpful cooking appliances, which includes stick blenders, water purifiers, pressure cookers, and pressure frying pans.
http://pleasanthillgrain.com

TAYLOR PRECISION PRODUCTS
This company sells a digital oven thermometer/timer.
www.taylorusa.com

Appendix B: Glossary

Anodize: To coat something, often metal such as aluminum, with a protective film.

Bake: A dry-heat method of cooking in which food is surrounded by heat at an even temperature.

Boil: Cooking method in which liquid is heated until it begins to change into a vapor.

Braise: A cooking method that uses both moist and dry heat. Typically the food is seared then cooked in a covered pot with liquid that covers $1/2 - 2/3$ of the food. Also referred to as pot-roasting.

Brine: A liquid mixture that usually combines sugar, salt, and other spices and is used to season meat by soaking it before cooking.

Broil: A dry-heat method of cooking in which food is placed directly under a heat source.

Butcher's twine: Thick cotton string used to truss meats, roasts, or tie bouquet garni, before cooking. Also referred to as kitchen twine.

Casserole: Any of a variety of deep-dish cooking vessels that can be used in the oven. This term also refers to the food cooked in these vessels.

Cast iron: Iron, typically pig iron and other alloying elements, which are melted down and then poured into a mold.

Chili pepper: The fruit of plants that are members of the nightshade family. Chili peppers come in many varieties, in heat levels from mild to very hot, and can be purchased fresh, dried, pickled, or powdered.

Chop: To cut food into small, uniform pieces (about $1/8 - 1/4$").

Creaming: The process of working food into a smooth paste. In baking it refers to blending butter and sugar into a uniform, often slightly fluffy, mixture.

Curry: A combination of spices used for cooking that can be a dry powder or paste. The types of spices vary depending on the type of cuisine.

Deep-fry: A cooking method in which food is cooked in heated oil.

Dice: To cut food into small, uniform cubes that can range in size from $1/4$" to $3/4$" depending on the recipe.

Ghee: Clarified butter commonly used in Indian cooking and for deep-frying.

Kaffir lime leaves: The fragrant leaves of the kaffir lime tree, which is native to India and Southeast Asia.

Mince: To finely chop food so that it is in pieces smaller than $1/8$".

Oxidation: The process by which oxygen combines with an element to change the appearance of that element.

Quart: A unit of liquid measurement in the United States that is equal to 2 pints or .946 liters.

Quinoa: An edible seed that is a good source of protein, fiber, and other nutrients.

Roast: A dry-heat cooking method in which hot air is used to cook the food. The heat can come from an oven, open flame, or other heat source.

Sear: The process of browning food by exposing it to high heat.

Slow cooking: A cooking method in which food is cooked for a long period at a moderate temperature. Often used for soups, stews, and tough cuts of meat.

Stainless steel: A steel alloy that does not corrode or rust.

Simmer: The temperature of a liquid while cooking that is just below the boiling point.

U.S./Metric Conversion Chart

VOLUME CONVERSIONS

U.S. Volume Measure	Metric Equivalent
⅛ teaspoon	0.5 milliliter
¼ teaspoon	1 milliliter
½ teaspoon	2 milliliters
1 teaspoon	5 milliliters
½ tablespoon	7 milliliters
1 tablespoon (3 teaspoons)	15 milliliters
2 tablespoons (1 fluid ounce)	30 milliliters
¼ cup (4 tablespoons)	60 milliliters
⅓ cup	90 milliliters
½ cup (4 fluid ounces)	125 milliliters
⅔ cup	160 milliliters
¾ cup (6 fluid ounces)	180 milliliters
1 cup (16 tablespoons)	250 milliliters
1 pint (2 cups)	500 milliliters
1 quart (4 cups)	1 liter (about)

WEIGHT CONVERSIONS

U.S. Weight Measure	Metric Equivalent
½ ounce	15 grams
1 ounce	30 grams
2 ounces	60 grams
3 ounces	85 grams
¼ pound (4 ounces)	115 grams
½ pound (8 ounces)	225 grams
¾ pound (12 ounces)	340 grams
1 pound (16 ounces)	454 grams

OVEN TEMPERATURE CONVERSIONS

Degrees Fahrenheit	Degrees Celsius
200 degrees F	95 degrees C
250 degrees F	120 degrees C
275 degrees F	135 degrees C
300 degrees F	150 degrees C
325 degrees F	160 degrees C
350 degrees F	180 degrees C
375 degrees F	190 degrees C
400 degrees F	205 degrees C
425 degrees F	220 degrees C
450 degrees F	230 degrees C

BAKING PAN SIZES

American	Metric
8 × 1½ inch round baking pan	20 × 4 cm cake tin
9 × 1½ inch round baking pan	23 × 3.5 cm cake tin
11 × 7 × 1½ inch baking pan	28 × 18 x 4 cm baking tin
13 × 9 × 2 inch baking pan	30 × 20 × 5 cm baking tin
2 quart rectangular baking dish	30 × 20 × 3 cm baking tin
15 × 10 × 2 inch baking pan	30 × 25 × 2 cm baking tin (Swiss roll tin)
9 inch pie plate	22 × 4 or 23 × 4 cm pie plate
7 or 8 inch springform pan	18 or 20 cm springform or loose bottom cake tin
9 × 5 × 3 inch loaf pan	23 × 13 × 7 cm or 2 lb narrow loaf or pate tin
1½ quart casserole	1.5 liter casserole
2 quart casserole	2 liter casserole

Index

Note: Page numbers in *italics* indicate photos.